Building Wealth and Living in Faith

Building Wealth
and
Living in Faith

A Father's Guide to Leaving Your Legacy

Mark A. Aho

The information contained in this book does not purport to be a complete description of the securities, markets, or developments referred to in this material. The information has been obtained from sources considered to be reliable, but we do not guarantee that the foregoing material is accurate or complete. Any information is not a complete summary or statement of all available data necessary for making an investment decision and does not constitute a recommendation to buy or sell any security. Past performance may not be indicative of future results. Any opinions stated are those of Mark A. Aho and not necessarily those of Raymond James or RJFS.

BUILDING WEALTH AND LIVING IN FAITH

A Father's Guide to Leaving Your Legacy

ISBN 978-1-5445-1132-0 *Hardcover*

978-1-5445-1133-7 *Paperback*

978-1-5445-1134-4 *Ebook*

This book is dedicated to my parents, Arne and June, who adopted me and guided me to a wonderful life. Also to my wife, Julie, and my children, Christina and Ross—treasured gifts from God.

Contents

Preface

My father didn't tell me how to live; he lived and let me watch him do it.

—CLARENCE KELLAND, AMERICAN WRITER

First of all, I want to thank you for reading this book. I'm deeply honored and truly blessed you have chosen to pick it up and spend some time with it. In these pages, you'll find the culmination of some of my most heartfelt thoughts, faith-based values, and financial wisdom gained throughout my lifetime as a successful financial planner, dedicated husband, loving father, and most importantly, child of God.

THE TIDE THAT RAISES ALL SHIPS

There is a poetic verse from an iconic and very popular folk song from 1974, written and performed by Harry Chapin, called "Cat's in the Cradle." It's all about how a boy emulates his father as he becomes a man. I'm reminded of it quite often when I think about my own kids and the children of my financial advisory clients as well. The words seem so familiar—they're just about etched into American pop culture now and for the foreseeable future.

The song starts with the child being born and learning to walk while his father's away, most likely at work or on a business trip of some kind. Throughout the middle of the song, the father misses various milestones due to his hectic work life and all-around busy schedule. It ends with the child grown up, and all of a sudden, the roles are reversed—the son no longer has time in his busy life to spend with his father. The beauty of the song is not only in its somewhat sad irony but also in the unmistakable parental bond that still exists in the undertones of the parent-child relationship. The boy grew up to be just like his dad, which speaks to this undeniable likeness, love, and respect between them. You might have to read between the lines a little to get that out of it, but it's there.

It's touching, heartwarming, and even a little tragic in its own beautiful way, but I also think it's very reflective of many similar relationships. In a weird way, that song is also a little inspiring to me because the message encapsulates my purpose for writing this book.

Understand how precious your time is with your children. They grow up fast, and before you know it, they're living lives of their own with their own careers, relationships, and families. It's important you seize the opportunity to effectively communicate some valuable life lessons with them while you still can. I know you're busy. There are long days at work; laundry, dishes, and other chores around the house that need to get done; and a lot of social events swirling around our lives. Nonetheless, you need to take advantage of that special time with your kids when you have it. It's during these times you can most readily share with them what you've learned about life, love, financial security, and God, among other things.

My hope is you will read this book, take it to heart, and share it with your children. I want it to be a positive influence (even if it's just a small one) in your continuing and developing relationship with your kids, your financial future, and the Lord. If the tide raises all ships, I'd like this book to be something of that nature for the people who read it. In other words, my goal is for this book to help you and your children live fuller, happier, and more financially secure lives.

Chance Encounters Serving as Lifelong Words of Wisdom

I learned one of my most valuable life lessons at the young

age of five during a chance encounter while running an errand at the bank with my mother. While I was waiting for her with my chin resting on the countertop, the bank manager walked by and caught my eye.

He asked me, "Do you realize if you save some of your money and you put it here, I'll give you more money back?"

Well, that whole concept just hit me like a ton of bricks! I was bored before he spoke to me, but the concept of saving officially grabbed my undivided attention and hasn't let go fifty-five years later.

As we were walking out of the bank, I remember incessantly tugging on my mom's skirt and pestering her about how we have to hurry up and get more money in the bank to save. I'm not sure exactly why the bank manager's words hit me the way they did, but the whole concept really made a sizable impression on me.

Maybe I started thinking about what I could get with the extra money I saved. Bubblegum was a penny per piece in those days. Maybe I figured if I put ten or twenty pennies in the bank, I could get an extra piece or two of bubblegum. It's also possible I was thinking about how much more money I could get back if I was frugal. Realistically, it was probably a little of both. Either way, I guess it seemed like a win-win to me.

I'm sixty years old now, and I remember that brief encounter with the bank manager like it was yesterday. I wonder if he realized how impactful his words were to me back then. We're so impressionable at that age, and I think it's important to remember that as adults. If your heart is filled with love and your words carry wisdom based on good intent, then you have such a profound ability to make a difference in the lives of your children and the world around you. We all have the ability to have a positive effect on somebody in our daily routines, similar to what the bank manager did for me that day. The power to favorably influence your world is within all of us to share with all of humanity.

We All Have a Calling

I was born and raised Roman Catholic in the town of Silver City, Michigan, and faith has always played a huge role in my life. After going to school in a nearby town called White Pine, I eventually went away to college at Northern Michigan University, which was about a two-and-a-half-hour ride from my hometown.

One weekend, while I was home visiting my folks, the priest from our parish took me aside and asked if I would consider joining the priesthood. Although I was honored by such a consideration, all I could think about was how I loved having girlfriends way too much to do that.

Therefore, when I was home again that summer, I politely turned down his offer. That decision haunted me a bit for the next thirty years because I felt like the Lord asked me to do something and I turned him down. I wouldn't quite call it guilt, but it was more than a little unsettling and disturbing to me, nonetheless.

Eventually, the Lord must have seen fit to alleviate me from my emotional conflict. It happened about nine years ago while I was doing a cursillo (a three-day, informal, layperson-organized retreat for all people to grow and ignite their faith) at a center called Mary Grove in the Upper Peninsula of Michigan. I got into a conversation with another priest while I was there, and I explained to him how that decision I made three decades ago had been troubling me ever since.

This particular priest was very insightful. He said, "You know, whatever you're doing in your profession, whatever you're doing in your life, you're doing God's work. You are where you need to be. Just think about all the people you talk to, all the review meetings you hold, and all the people who come to you for advice. How you go about doing those things is doing what the Lord needs you to do."

That made so much sense to me, and I encourage you to heed those words of wisdom as well, because you have the power to make a difference simply by doing whatever it is you do to the best of your abilities every day. That sentiment might sound overly simplified, but it's true. After all, as Leonardo da Vinci said, "Simplicity is the ultimate form of sophistication." I would say that priest's philosophy is so simplistically sophisticated, it's beautiful—perhaps, even godly.

Develop a Value System

Developing a value system is a great way to ensure you do whatever it is you do every day to the best of your ability. It also guarantees each action you take throughout your lifetime aligns with the person you want to be. By developing such a system, you'll find many other aspects of your life fall into place as well. This requires nothing more than a piece of paper and a pen.

What exactly is a value system? I stumbled on this concept early in my working career about twenty-seven years ago when I was studying the commonalities of successful people. A value system is a list of personal values to live by, and it's never too late or too early to start one. You could start yours at twenty-five, thirty-five, fifty, or any age. The idea actually originated back in the 1700s with Ben Franklin, and it's a wonderful way to gauge whether you're living life the way you really want to.

How do you know if your value system is true? That answer

is easy—it won't change. The same list I originally comprised over twenty-seven years ago still holds true today. None of those values I initially wrote down have changed. I encourage you to do the same thing and hold yourself to your own unique system.

The individual values are going to be different for everybody, but I've listed mine here to get you jump-started on your own system in case you need it. I urge you to be honest with yourself and take the time to write up this list based on your own standards and good intentions. Your list could be much shorter or longer, but length is of no importance.

What is important is that they correctly describe the way you want to live your life. Keep this list tucked away in a safe place and read them every day for a while if you need to. You'll notice whether what you write down is true, they won't change over time, because they truly identify who you have become.

Just for reference, this is what mine looked like when I wrote it many years ago. Every once in a while, when I need to be reminded of what's truly important to me, I take my value list out of the desk drawer I keep it in and read it again.

1. **Continue to develop my relationship with God and Jesus:** Learn all I can about Jesus by reading the Bible and praying. Strive to walk in his ways.
2. **Be a good husband to my wife, Julie:** Always treat her with the highest regard. Be empathetic to her daily duties and try to put myself in her place to understand what she's going through. Always maintain complete and open communication with her. Remember to think about her before I make any decisions in life. Show her daily how much I love her and always take care of her emotionally and physically. Always be prepared to give my life for her.
3. **Be a good father to my children:** Spend quality time with my children. Participate daily in as many events as possible. Show them how much I love them, daily. Teach them to be responsible citizens of this country and the world. Slow down my busy world to talk to and listen to these precious children. Always be there for them and let them know they can always depend on me.
4. **Maintain good physical and mental health:** Maintain a good diet. Do not eat or drink to dullness. Do not drink alcoholic beverages to excess. Exercise daily. To stay healthy mentally, I will always talk about my problems and emotions with someone I trust and seek advice for anything that troubles me.
5. **Become financially independent and self-reliant:** Work daily to improve my work and strive for excellence. Develop a good idea that will harbor financial independence.
6. **Be optimistic:** Always look at the glass as half full, instead of half empty.
7. **Be honest:** Always tell the truth. Develop open relationships with everybody.
8. **Be frugal:** Spend only on needed items and when it does some good for somebody.
9. **Be competent:** Always strive to know the subject matter I am responsible for. Never claim to be all-knowing in areas I'm not properly prepared for or educated in.
10. **Grow intellectually:** Always strive to learn more about my subject matters of interest, and in subject matters I need to know more about.
11. **Live by the Golden Rule (silence, sincerity, and justice):** Treat others the way I want to be treated. Speak not but what may benefit others or myself. Avoid trifling conversation. And wrong nobody by doing injuries.
12. **Have confidence and integrity:** Live confidently, not in fear. Maintain strong integrity.

There is a catch with writing down a list of core values, which is: you will have to deny yourself something at some point in your lifetime.

That's the challenging aspect of this exercise for a lot of people. It's okay—we're all human, and we're all going to make mistakes. However, in order for this to be a truly effective exercise, you need to abide by these rules as often as possible. For instance, one of my core values is to grow intellectually. That means periodically I have to step outside of my comfort zone and read something not ordinarily in my wheelhouse. I need to expand my intelligence to areas with which I'm not already familiar. Your list may present different challenges, but that makes it valuable and worth doing.

Introduction

Four Blessings

Adopting one child won't change the world. But for that child, the world will change.

—UNKNOWN

At sixty years of age now, I've had considerable time to reflect on the many fulfilling aspects of my life, which is the principle reason I'm writing this book:

- I have a wonderful marriage with an amazing woman.
- I have a son and daughter who are both sources of tremendous joy for me.
- I've had the opportunity to work and socialize with some truly inspiring individuals.
- I run a successful financial planning practice in the Upper Peninsula of Michigan.

I am thankful for too many things to be able to list them all. Life has certainly presented its challenges at various times, but I've gotten through them all with faith. In fact, the reason I am as fulfilled, happy, and successful as I am can all be attributed to four blessings I received early in life to help me become who I am today:

1. The gift of life
2. The Good Will Farm
3. Adoption
4. My adoptive family

The next few pages will detail how each of these blessings has positively affected my life. I'm grateful for each one, and by reading about them, I hope you'll find some blessings in your own life to be used as positive energy to build upon as well.

Blessing #1: The Gift of Life

Adversity can mean different things to different people. It all depends on your perspective. In my case, adversity relates to my birth mother because she faced a tremendous amount of it during her pregnancy with me.

Having a baby was going to be difficult at best for her because she had almost no support. She lived on bread and lard for sustenance because she was incredibly poor, and my birth father denied he ever had anything to do with her. In other words, if ever there was a baby to abort, it was me.

Fortunately, she faced that adversity head-on, stared it down, and overcame it all to give me life. That realization, along with my life principles and values, has made me a big advocate of the pro-life ideology. In today's highly energized proabortion movement, I probably would have been aborted. I would never have been given the gift of seeing all the good around me throughout my lifetime. Therefore, how could I not be pro-life?

Blessing #2: The Good Will Farm

It might seem strange to think of something like an orphanage as a blessing, but I think that's an accurate description in my case. My birthmother knew leaving me with the wonderfully altruistic people of the Good Will Farm was the right thing to do for both of us.

Lesser people merely going through the motions in their jobs there could have impacted my life in a very negative way. But the people who worked there served the Lord admirably by performing their jobs to the absolute best of their abilities. That simple act guided me purposefully to the life of love and happiness I still have today. What a blessing those hardworking, well-intentioned people at the Good Will Farm were indeed.

I'm sure my birthmother and I would have loved each other very much, but she was facing so much adversity that keeping me would have been difficult, and who knows what would have happened to me from there.

In her infinite wisdom, she chose a different path for me. Because of her foresight in bringing me to the Good Will Farm, fate and the Lord intervened, and I was taken in by my adoptive family, who went on to bless me with so much more.

Blessing #3: Adoption

So much about adoption is misinterpreted by people unfamiliar with its dynamics. Many people think it's an act riddled with carelessness and selfishness. In reality, it's just the opposite.

Adoption is an act done with deep consideration and valiant selflessness. Most birth mothers don't want to give their babies to someone else, but they do because they know it's the best thing for the baby.

I'm told my birth mother didn't want to place me for adoption, but out of love, care, and selflessness, she did it anyway, and it was definitely the right thing to do. The Good Will Farm may have been a blessing in disguise, but it was definitely a blessing.

I was extremely blessed. I ended up being taken in by two loving, caring people with strong character and high morals. When I look back on the adversity my birth mother faced and the opportunity for a happy life I was subsequently given by my parents who raised me, I'm reminded of a short story by Loren Eiseley, called "The Star Thrower."

It's a story about an old man and a boy who see things a little differently. They're on a beach that is significantly covered with starfish, and the boy keeps picking them up to throw them back in the ocean. This looks a little strange to the old man, so he asks the boy why he is doing such a thing. When the boy responds that it's hot out and the starfish will die if he doesn't, the man exclaims that there must be 10,000 starfish on the beach and the boy won't possibly be able to make much of a difference. The boy then throws another one back in the water and says something like, "Well, it sure made a difference to that one!"

At least, that is my best recollection of the story. I've always thought of myself as that starfish. I like to think my birth mother threw me back into the ocean and gave me another chance at life.

When my parents adopted me as an infant through the Good Will Farm, they were moving from Detroit, Michigan, to the Upper Peninsula area, where I eventually grew up. They already had one daughter, and they were trying to have another child, but my mother kept having miscarriages.

My mother always said my adoption happened so fast they weren't prepared to have me right away. They had no supplies for me until a nice neighbor couple, Jimmy and Doris Spolarich, gave them a lot of things babies need, like a crib for me to sleep in and some clothes to wear.

Through the accelerated pace of bringing me into the family, my parents never missed a beat. I always knew they loved me from day one. They used to introduce me by saying something like, "This is our son, Mark. We adopted him, and he is very special to us." That way, I learned to be proud of my adoption.

You have the ability to make something special for somebody in your life too. All you have to do is share your time and love. It doesn't have to involve something as big as adopting a child. Every day, you have a chance to perform a random act of kindness for someone that will make a big difference in their lives. You never know what kind of impact you're having by throwing a starfish back into the ocean or saying something wise to an impressionable youngster at the bank. I thank God for those gifts every day.

Blessing #4: Adoptive Family

Maybe you're thinking adoptive family is a repetitive concept because I've already discussed, in detail, how blessed I was that my mother and father adopted me. That part is true, but when I add the word "family" to the term, it takes on an even deeper level and more substantial meaning.

Mom and Dad taught me all kinds of valuable lessons, which I'm going to discuss in the next section, but my adoptive family includes more than just them. I also have a wonderful sister who is four years older than I am. I grew up with her, and probably drove her a little crazy sometimes, as younger brothers usually do. However, through her never-ending patience, inherent kindness, and eternal love, she understood I looked up to her and just wanted to be with her. As a result, we were always very close and remain that way today.

My adoptive family extends much farther than I ever even realized, because my father was one of sixteen kids, and thirteen of them were still alive while I was growing up. I also had two uncles and another aunt on my mother's side. Somehow, they all played big roles in my development, especially during my younger years. Believe it or not, I felt very close to each and every one of them. In fact, I don't know if they realized how much I loved them.

My extended family was such a big part of my life. Whenever they visited, it seemed like such a joyous occasion. Usually my dad and I were out working somewhere. Maybe we were out installing a septic system with our shovels firmly entrenched in the ground or on the rooftop building a new roof, but whenever one of my aunts or uncles arrived, we would leave our shovels wherever they were and greet them warmly. Then, my mom would bring out coffee and cookies and whatever other treats might be nice to share with our family, and it was officially visiting time. Work was halted until the visiting was finished, because it was time to be with these very special people.

All of my aunts and uncles were very important to me, but none of them were a bigger part of my life than my dear Aunt Madeline, or Auntie Mad, as I liked to call her. She was always so warm and loving to me.

My house was always so busy because my mom and dad shared a wonderful entrepreneurial spirit. Also, as I said before, I spent a lot of my time getting my hands dirty working with my dad, and I learned so many valuable things. So whenever I went over Auntie Mad's house, the first thing she did was put me in the bathtub to clean me up a little. Then, she would usually offer me all kinds of cookies and pies, too, because she was very domestic and always had something good in the oven.

Auntie Mad had six kids and lived only a block or two

away from my school in White Pine. I was at her house so often it was almost like I was her seventh child. We used to laugh about that a lot in our family. Of course, one of the reasons I was at her house so much was because I was very close to one of her sons, named Patrick. He and I were good friends throughout our childhood and adolescent years. He's always been like a brother to me, and we remain very close today. By the way, Auntie Mad is eighty-seven years young today and is still just as kind and caring as ever. In fact, she probably has a batch of cookies in the oven right now.

My uncle Reuben is someone I remember in a particularly fond way. He was always jolly and was a genuinely good guy. I wish I would have taken some time as a kid to tell him how special he was to me and how much I loved him. Of course, you don't really think about stuff like that when you're a kid.

The best part about this big, happy family of mine is nobody in it ever considered me adopted. I was just part of the family. There were no lines drawn or distinctions made. I was just Mark to all those supportive aunts and uncles, my wonderful sister, and my loving parents.

Many of us have these wonderfully significant people in our lives who extend so much of their love and compassion to others. They could be aunts and uncles, grandparents, or even very friendly neighbors. That level of closeness can come from all walks of life, but we need to recognize it before it's too late. It's only natural for a child or an adolescent to not fully realize how important these people can be until we get older. If you're a parent reading this, I urge you to express to your children how precious this time in their lives is with their extended family.

The Core Lessons My Parents Shared with Me

With love at the heart of it all, my parents imparted some core lessons throughout my childhood and adolescence. These four valuable teachings can provide a sound foundation for anyone looking to experience a richer, more satisfying life.

1. Hard work
2. Faith
3. Belief in the future
4. An entrepreneurial spirit

The next few pages are going to explain in greater detail how these four lessons shaped my personality and played a significant role in who I am today. Maybe by reading these lessons, you'll uncover some aspects of your childhood, adolescence, or even younger adult years that you can use to build even more positive energy from the four blessings we discussed earlier.

Lesson #1: Hard Work

My mother and father both worked hard throughout their lives. Dad was a painter at a copper mine, but he was always working on something outside of that job too. He and my mother owned and operated some motel-style cabins as an entrepreneurial endeavor, and my dad was always either building or fixing something for that business.

My Dad: At Work, Seven Days a Week

Dad grew up on a small dairy farm near the city of Hancock, Michigan, and if you grow up on a farm, you're no stranger to hard work. Even with fifteen brothers and sisters, there were still plenty of chores for everybody to do all day, every day.

The copper mine was where my dad worked his day job, Monday through Friday, from 7:00 a.m. to 3:00 p.m. He would get home around 3:30 p.m., have dinner, and take a twenty-minute catnap. Then he was off to work on the cabins they owned, which I helped him with a lot. He did the painting, plumbing, electrical, and basic construction on the buildings until about 10:00 p.m. on weeknights. On the weekends, when he wasn't working at the copper mine, he would exclusively do the property maintenance work around the cabins.

I probably didn't think much about it at the time, but when

I look back on those days of helping my dad with work, I realize how fortunate I was to have spent that time with him. In retrospect, I learned everything I needed to know about owning a house too. Now, I can do everything from rewiring the electrical in a home to replacing the roof and everything in between.

I played a lot of sports as a kid—football in the fall, basketball in the winter, and track and field in the spring. I loved all those sports, but no matter what I did during the day, my dad always expected me to help him work afterward, even on weekends. Back then, I might have thought I was missing out on some activities when my friends were going out to a lot of social events and having fun. But now I realize how valuable that time working with my dad was, and I'm very grateful for it.

What do you think happened when I came home for the weekends in college? That's right, we had work to do. In fact, my dad and I built an entire restaurant while I was in college. We didn't have enough money to contract any of that work out, so we did all the construction and repair work ourselves—the kitchen, the dining room, you name it.

Even with the demands of all this work on my schedule, I still found time for summer jobs to help pay for school. In fact, I paid for almost my entire college education that way. My dad taught me about the value of hard work at a young age and kept reinforcing the idea throughout my time with him. With hard work, he taught me that you could build a restaurant, maintain a home, even pay for a college education, and who knows what else?

My Mom: The Extroverted Entrepreneurial Spirit

Mom was a hard worker too—she just had a different skill set. Whereas my dad was very introverted and put his energy into physical things, my mom was very extroverted. She used to meet and greet everybody who came to their cabins. She loved the hospitality involved with that business, and she was very good at it too, which rubbed off on me a bit.

In a way, I got the best of both worlds when it came to learning about hard work. My dad taught me about physical labor and how to build things, but my mom taught me about people, which is also a very valuable skill.

Between the work with my father and the time I spent with my mom talking to guests and getting them what they needed, I didn't have time for much else. If they say idle hands are the devil's workshop, then you could say I never found myself in the devil's workshop, and that's a really good thing for anyone of any age.

Lesson #2: Faith

My dad was a non-practicing Apostolic Lutheran and my mom was a Roman Catholic. She took me to church every Sunday while my dad—you guessed it—worked. My mom's involvement in the church was a big influence in establishing and maintaining my own faith.

I don't judge anyone for their views on faith or religion. Everyone is entitled to believe what they want to believe, and it's part of being human to ask questions like, "Is there really a God?" But I've always held very tightly on to my faith and religion. It works for me and plays a central role in who I am today. I love God and all he has done for humanity—that will never change.

God loves all faiths and all churches. To degrade one religion that praises him and professes love among your fellow humans is almost sinful. That ideology was a bit of a revelation for me three to four years ago.

My wife is Lutheran and I'm Roman Catholic, and after many conversations throughout our beautiful marriage, we came to the conclusion, together, that all Christian religions point to Christ and God. From those talks over the years, our marriage grew even fuller and more beautiful once we came to peace with this realization.

In any marriage, it's important to not get caught up in

semantics or dogma. We should always support our partner's faith journey. That support through love and devotion is far more important than debating the principles of one religion over another.

Lesson #3: Belief in the Future

My faith extends to a belief in the future of humanity's ability to make the world a better place. It's not healthy or productive to dwell on negative actions of the past. Regret is not something we should waste our energies on because it doesn't help us to contribute to a better future. If you do that, you're only making things worse. The way I see it, you can choose to live optimistically positive or pessimistically negative.

The Negative Space

Most people live in either a negatively or positively influenced space. People who live in the negative space think the world is against them and there's no sense in trying to make things better. It's a glass-half-empty mindset that seems like such a sad place to waste too much of your precious time.

I don't understand people who choose pessimism over optimism. The negative space is so devoid of hope and makes it difficult—almost impossible—for love to fill their hearts. That's not to say those with a negative mindset are incapable of love. Of course they are, but I think they miss out on a lot of love and happiness because they're too busy dwelling on negative things. Growth in any aspect becomes challenging at best if you have little hope for the future.

The Positive (Transformative) Space

The transformative space starts with being optimistic about what lies ahead. By thinking positively and believing in the future, you can change things and grow spiritually, mentally, physically, and financially. You just need faith—faith in God, faith in your fellow human beings, and faith in yourself.

Sometimes it's hard to wake up in the morning, turn on the news, and not have a pessimistic view of the day because we're constantly bombarded with so much negativity. If that's a problem, then I suggest turning off the television or putting it on a channel that has more of an upbeat message.

Organizations are helping starving people all over the world.

Sick children are getting life-saving organ transplants and other surgical procedures that were only a dream fifteen years ago.

Premature babies who weigh one or two pounds at birth are now surviving. Those little miracles had almost no chance at survival fifteen years ago.

Miracles are happening all around us. On a smaller scale, I see at least five to ten acts of random kindness every day, but you need to have the right mindset to recognize them when you see them.

Spirituality is a different ball of yarn to unravel in the transformative space. It's so easy to get caught up in the negativity of the news these days. A lot of protest, anger, hatred, and violence are publicized every day in the mainstream media.

A lack of faith can cloud your financial decision-making, as well as your life choices. Many times, a client will tell me they think there's nothing out there left to invest in, that all the good ideas have been taken. That's so categorically incorrect. I spend the rest of our meeting convincing them of the opposite. For some reason, they must have been weighted down with negativity. My job at that point is to transform them. I need to get them back into a mindset that enables growth and fosters prosperity. I usually start by sharing with them all the reasons to be optimistic about the future.

For instance, genome mapping is probably going to show

us our likelihood of developing cancer, adult-onset diabetes, ALS, and probably every other illness that has plagued humanity since our existence on Earth. Right now, it's expensive, so it's reserved for people with a lot of disposable income. Industry experts predict the procedure will get affordable at some point. Maybe health insurance companies will start covering the procedure someday, which would translate to tremendous savings in health care. By the time you read this, it may be much less expensive, and new breakthroughs may have occurred. This is a fast-paced development.

There are so many exciting, emerging technologies to feel good about in the future. Just think about all the innovations going on in the energy and automobile industries. No matter what, we're going from coal to natural gas at some point in the near future. Cars are going from gas to electric because battery technology is far superior. And that's just a small sampling of what's coming. There's so much more to look forward to that could provide great reasons to be optimistic about future investments and financial planning.

There's so much good in the world and there are so many reasons to believe in the future. All you have to do is stop dwelling on the past, focus on the present moment you can control, and have faith in the future.

Lesson #4: Entrepreneurial Spirit

My parents instilled the importance of an entrepreneurial spirit in me at a pretty young age. I saw how hard they worked in multiple jobs to make ends meet, and I knew early on how important it was to save. In a lot of ways, the example they set gave me a leg up in my career and my lifestyle.

Just watching the way my mom dealt with all of our motel guests, her remarkable gift for conversation with everyone who came to our door, and the way my dad worked morning, noon, and night to keep up with the maintenance was very inspirational to me.

Being accountable for your own financial well-being as an entrepreneur can be motivating and satisfying in many ways. I encourage you to accept a path of entrepreneurialism if it's in you. If you have a calling to make your own business work, do it while you're young because youth is a tremendous opportunity for all of us, and an entrepreneurial spirit is a wonderful gift to use while you still have the opportunity.

If you're part of a young married couple and one of you has an entrepreneurial spirit, it's important for your spouse to embrace and support it. Entrepreneurialism doesn't always involve one success after another. Failure is a big part of it. How you respond to failure will play a big role in determining your ultimate success. In order to respond favorably, you're going to need the support of your significant other to get through it and persevere.

A Rare Find

The primary reason I decided to write this book was because I had so much I wanted to share and to tell my children, Christina and Ross. These precious children mean the world to me. Even though I talk with them a lot, I realized they needed to have something in writing to absorb these messages about life as they were able to on their own schedule and time.

I also wanted to share these messages with all my clients' children. For they've also said to me many times, "I wish my kids were here to hear your message." So for my kids, your kids, and hopefully anyone who picks up this book, may your faith grow and carry you to new heights you never thought possible.

In this book, I will share simple lessons to provide the peace of mind that comes from having a secure financial future.

Hopefully, you will find this book to be one of a kind, a rare literary work that doesn't fit into any one category. Although I've included many insights about building wealth, I've also left plenty of thoughts about the importance of faith and living a fulfilled life of love and purpose. In a perfect world, this book would be found under the section titled "Financial Self-Help Spirituality." Understanding that section doesn't exist, if this book helps you to grow even the slightest bit in any of those categories, then no matter what section it's in, I will have done my job.

Chapter One

The Story Changes, but Truths Remain

To the one who has, more will be given; from the one who has not, even what he has will be taken away.

—MARK 4:14–25

This quote from the book of Mark can confound a lot of folks. Usually, it causes a reaction like, "What do you mean? You're going to give the rich guy even more than he already has? That makes no sense." The biggest paradox surrounding the verse is that most people relate it to material possessions like money; however, I think it has more to do with faith than anything else.

I interpret it to mean those who have a lot of faith will be rewarded with even more of it. Positive energy naturally breeds more positive energy. Conversely, those with little faith will probably have even that taken away from them because they're not good stewards. Their mind is too cluttered with negative energy for faith to prosper.

Another paradoxical section from the book of Mark is the verses about Jesus's return to his hometown. The Bible distinctly mentions very few miracles happened during that visit because the people had such little faith. At first glance, this section reads somewhat dispiritedly, because his hometown, a place that could use a few miracles, lacked the necessary faith for those miracles to occur.

Miracles happen frequently in other sections of the Bible, and it's because those people who were blind or lame and touched Jesus's cloak were healed due to their strong faith. Similarly, if you have faith in your own ability to grow spiritually and financially, it will happen. From a financial perspective, you also need to have good intentions about wealth creation. If you have both faith and a good heart with right intent, there's no reason your wealth can't grow continuously throughout your lifetime.

Four More Lessons

That quote from the book of Mark is so impactful to me, and it made me think a lot about what it's trying to teach us beyond the surface of its words. After reflecting on the quote for a while, I realize it taught me about four more lessons:

1. Humility
2. Discipline
3. Responsibility to family
4. Tending to your own garden

The next few pages discuss how these four lessons have been applied to my life to create a more secure financial future, greater purpose, and a fuller life. Hopefully, you will find a way to acquire some of the same good fortune by understanding how they've helped me.

Humility

My failures generated the greatest growth in my life, painfully so and, yes, full of humility. The first time I started in the financial business, I walked throughout my city and knocked on as many doors as I could to introduce myself in an attempt to drum up enough business to survive. That initial venture was not successful, but with the support of my loving wife, I was able to get through it.

The last thing I wanted to do when I independently set out to control my own business destiny was fail. The result was very embarrassing, but it taught me some great life lessons in the process. All of them had humility at the center.

Eventually, I gathered my confidence back, and with Julie's support, many years later, I was able to successfully venture out on my own entrepreneurial endeavor in the financial world for the second time. This time, with much greater success that I still appreciate today. However, I don't think any of it would have been possible without the lessons I learned in humility from many years before. It was hard to realize it at the time, but my initial failure really provided me with a wonderful opportunity to learn and grow.

If you're looking for a lesson in humility without the stress of financial setbacks, consider the game of golf. Golf is a tremendously humbling game. It's natural for most of us to step onto the first tee box and think our self-worth depends on our first tee shot. It doesn't, but when we're first starting out, inevitably, there's going to be a few that go into the rough about twenty-five yards away after a vicious swing at the ball. Keep playing though, because after a while, those duffs that go dribbling come around less often, and some tried and true lasers down the middle of the fairway will begin to surface—as long as you accept the lesson in humility from those initial experiences while learning the game.

Through humility and failure is how you learn the most. If you don't pick yourself up after a failed business venture or a duffed tee-shot, that's when failure triumphs. When you get up, you're stronger, and you triumph with the Lord at your side.

Discipline

I know a lot of wonderful people whom I love dearly, and they've never built any wealth in their entire lives. That is fine for them, but for the people who want to build wealth and strive to make work optional as soon as possible, discipline is required.

Discipline might be much easier to acquire in your more formative years of childhood or adolescence. It's never too late to try, however, because with God in your heart, anything is possible.

Usually, the people who inherit money or win it in the lottery spend it as fast as they can collect it. Not only do they spend what they inherit or win, but many times, they indebt themselves even further. They lack the necessary discipline that comes from the efforts of creatively earning this amount of money on their own from things like hard work and strong faith to make their good fortune last.

Discipline goes back to having a value system to keep you in line. You have to deny yourself something once in a while to retain your values. In the long run, this will help you become very financially and spiritually secure.

Even if discipline wasn't ingrained into you during your childhood, establishing an honest and true value system can help you to instill it at any age.

Responsibility to Family

If I don't somehow create some wealth for myself, how am I going to be able to financially help anybody else? As a provider, I always wanted to raise the life of my wife by providing her with stability. That's the first level of responsible financial planning, and I'm sure there are many more people who share that same value. Know the why before you figure out the how. In other words, understand the reasons you want to be able to do certain things with your wealth and you can figure out how to do them afterward.

The second level is concerned with your children. If kids are involved, you need to provide for them in a safe manner while ensuring they have ample opportunities to create their own savings and wealth. If you're not creating those things, then how do you expect them to be able to? Kids learn a lot from their parents. Sure, they learn plenty from school, and probably too much from their friends, but their parents are the ones who can instill some sensible strategies for ongoing success. I suggest you lead by example and show your children how to save and create wealth.

There is a third level of responsibility that goes beyond

your spouse and children. It goes to your aging parents and perhaps other family members in need, like aunts and uncles. The circle of life usually involves children reaching adulthood as their parents enter their senior years. This is when the tables are turned as far as care goes. All of a sudden, kids need to monitor the physical, mental, and financial well-being of their parents. It becomes your child's turn to hopefully have the resources necessary to care for their parents.

I was blessed enough with my own wealth creation to be able to buy a car for my mother not too long ago. She was saving a small pension for quite a while and had planned to buy a car with it. When she showed up at the dealer, they told her it was already paid for. She almost fell over, but I got so much fulfillment from being able to do that for her, I felt like I got the bigger gift. My heart jumped for joy when I was able to do that, just like it does when I have enough savings to do something really nice for my kids.

If you're good enough in your financial planning to account for those three levels of familial need, there could be a fourth level you want to address, which is charitable contributions. Some of us who are truly blessed from a financial perspective have the ability to help others who aren't related to us in any way.

Think about people like Bill and Melinda Gates and Warren

Buffet who have used their extreme wealth to help others around the world who they don't even know. The ability to help others serves the dual purpose of allowing you to grow spiritually to feel better about the wealth you've created while knowing it has gone to a philanthropic and altruistic purpose.

It's wonderfully beneficial to humanity when someone creates enough wealth—like Bill Gates—to give away nearly all of his fortune. I'm not sure what the real dollar value is for his net worth, but let's say he's worth $75 billion and he gives away $74 billion. Do you think he might be able to eke out his life with just $1 billion? Of course, he can! But that's because he created so much wealth in his lifetime that he can not only live extremely comfortably, but he can use his money for the greater good as well. He's fulfilling a wonderfully selfless responsibility to the rest of humanity.

Tending to Your Own Garden

Another piece of wisdom I've paid great attention to in my lifetime is a notion that if you tend your garden responsibly, it will grow, and it doesn't matter what type of garden or how big it is.

That garden could be an exclusively spiritual one, with savings and financial well-being playing no role in its growth. Some of the happiest people on Earth don't have a lot of money or any material possessions to speak of. They're just happy because they're tending a garden that helps all the people they touch in their lives. They may not be financially wealthy or even stable, but they are spiritually and soulfully rich.

If you have a million dollars in the bank and you tend to it well, it may grow to $2 million, $5 million, or who knows how much more. By the same token, if you have only $10,000 in the bank, as long as you mindfully tend to it, that can grow as well. You can't, however, make your $10,000 grow into $100,000 or your $1 million grow into more millions unless you tend to it properly. If you neglect your garden, it will die—$1 million will shrivel down to $100,000, and $10,000 will emaciate away to nothing in almost no time at all.

What does it take to tend to your garden properly?

The answer is easy—it's faith. In my mind, faith is the driving force behind everything you do in life. If God is in your heart, your words, and your actions, then your garden will grow in many ways.

Money Is Not the Root of All Evil. Greed Is

Some people believe creating wealth is bad or the devil's

work. If you create wealth honorably or have good intentions, then you will have done God's will.

Some people think they can let their garden tend itself. For instance, a person of pure faith may have the mindset that God will provide for them, and it's certainly fine to feel that way. They might look at a biblical verse and say something like, "You don't need to fill your silos full of corn and wheat, nor do you need to construct more buildings to store earthly treasures because God will provide for you just like he does for the birds and the animals." Whereas I accept that philosophy wholeheartedly, if you look a little more deeply, you'll see the tremendous good that can come from your singular creation of wealth. I don't think of the indulgences wealth can afford someone, but I see the abundances it can create for people around them many years after they're gone.

Many people have the misconception that money is the root of all evil. I don't think that's true at all. There's a distinction to be made between the terms "money" and "greed." They are vastly different entities. Money is merely a tool to be used for many good purposes. It can be used to educate, feed, provide shelter, and many other wonderful necessities.

The love of money is where greed rears its ugly head. Creating wealth just to watch your silos fill with corn and wheat or, in more modern-day circumstances, just to watch your bank accounts add up with no good intentions or reasonable purpose for their use is a problem.

Later on, I'm going to talk about the six principles of investor behavior. Greed, however, is a principle to be wary of. Similar to fear, which can cripple your decision-making into non-decisions, where you end up doing nothing and watching the world prosper around you, greed can influence you to make foolhardy decisions.

A good example of how greed can be problematic took place in the late 1990s. I lost many clients in those days because people got tempted by some of the hot start-ups. The idea of sustainable growth and faith in our basic formula of stocks, bonds, cash, and diversification was cast aside for the high-flying technology companies. From 1997 to 1999, some of my clients were arguing that we were missing the boat. So many of those companies had escalating stock prices with virtually zero earnings. It was unfounded optimism in unproven products.

Faith in the future is good, but blindly throwing all your hard-earned money into technology that hasn't yet produced anything of value is what happens when greed takes over. People saw the get-rich-quick illusion and wanted to jump in. What happened? In 2000, the dot-com bubble burst. Investors who were disproportionately heavy into those stocks got absolutely crushed.

Compliance Note: Companies engaged in business related to a specific sector are subject to fierce competition, and their products and services may be subject to rapid obsolescence. There are additional risks associated with investing in an individual sector, including limited diversification.

Make Choices That Reflect Your Values and Your Faith

One way to look at making investment choices that reflect your values and faith is in terms of social responsibility. That may mean not investing in companies that make bombs or other military weapons. It might mean not investing in alcohol or tobacco companies because of a social conscience. These are very noble intentions, and you have the right to invest only in companies you deem worthy of your money. That's more of a values perspective.

From a faith perspective, it comes down to deciding whether to save in the first place. When I talk about faith in this context, I'm referring to a faith that is larger than just the Dow Jones Industrial Average, real estate prices, or the labor market. I'm referring to faith in the future of this Earth and God. Some people choose not to save, which is okay. It's not what I would recommend, but it's their choice. Most of those people back up their viewpoint by saying they don't trust the markets and they don't want to live their lives watching their investments going up and down. I respect their viewpoint, but I think if those same people had a deeper understanding of faith, they would think differently.

Start Now and Be Patient

If you have the necessary faith in the future to start saving and investing, you have to start someplace. If you're young and just starting out, the first thing you should do is separate your checking account from your savings.

It's an amazing thing, but if you put everything in checking, by the end of every month, that money will have pulled a Houdini act—it will disappear. Whereas if you separate some of it instead, whatever you put in savings will grow. Start by putting just 10 percent of your income into a savings account and see what happens.

Once you're able to put that money away without causing any problems, you should start prioritizing things you need. Deny yourself the superfluous items. Then, maybe you discover you can save 12 or even 16 percent. When you discover you can save some money and adjust your lifestyle to meet your savings need, then you can decide how to invest that money.

401(K) PLANS

Most companies today offer a matching 401(k) plan, which can be a great option to save for retirement.

If you're not familiar with a 401(k), it's a plan that allows employees to save before- and after-tax dollars, while in many cases, the corporation matches a certain percentage of the employees' pay—usually around 4 to 6 percent. The traditional version of a 401(k) is a before-tax savings plan, while the 401(k) Roth is an after-tax savings plan.

My advice regarding 401(k) plans is to put in as much as you possibly can. Not doing at least what the company match is would be foolish because it's turning down extra pay from the company. If they're offering that money and if you don't put your percentage in, the corporation most likely won't provide any match. In other words, it's a benefit that's being provided to you. At least put in what the company will match, and the more you can put in after that, the better off you could be.

Inevitably, once people start to see their savings grow, they start worrying about the volatility of the markets. What happens to my money if 2008 occurs all over again? What happens if something "too big to fail," fails again? If you're young, that's not such a bad thing. In fact, it could be a good thing in the long run.

When the market drops, you need to be patient and stay in it long enough to meet your long-term goals. Moving money in and out in an attempt to time the market won't work. Equities will most likely provide a rewarding return by just staying in the market. You just need to make sure you don't panic and withdraw your funds during the downward swing so your investments are still there for the next uptick.

Although the bursting of the dot-com bubble in 2000 and the subprime mortgage crisis of 2008 both seemed like fatal economic events at the time, those who stayed with their initial plan reaped the rewards of the recovery due to their patience and discipline.

Sir John Templeton, who was a Rhodes Scholar, a Knight Bachelor, and an American-born British investor, had a lot of famous quotes, but one of his most famous is: "The four most expensive words in the English language are, 'This time it's different.'"

The market has historically always come back. Don't be afraid. Everybody feared it would be different in 2008, but it wasn't. Don't let those four words be expensive for you. Keep investing because factually, the market has been on an upward growth march since it started over two hundred years ago, and there's no reason for that to change over the next two hundred years.

Compliance Note: There is no assurance that any investment strategy will be successful. Investing involves risk, and investors may incur a profit or a loss. Asset allocation and diversification do not ensure a profit or protect against a loss. Past performance is not indicative of future results.

Don't Be Afraid

Most of my clients are not afraid of investing. They have some extrinsic faith in the future, the patience to wait out a down market, and the discipline to keep saving. They come to me either early in their life with a desire to create wealth—generally to make work optional at some point in their future—or they had a life event that left them a substantial amount of money, they sold a business, received an inheritance, or might be going through a divorce. Some have had equities most of their lives, not understanding how things may work out in retirement.

Especially while you're young, if you're afraid to invest or assume some risk in those investments, you could be missing the opportunity for your financial garden to grow quite a bit. For example, I've seen many newly retired clients at age sixty-five or sixty-six who have lived their lives with a fear of investing. They invested all their money in low return investments such as bonds and cash. After talking to them, I started to unpeel the layers of the onion representing their phobia of the market. The confounding part of this is these people were lifelong savers, but they were just deathly afraid of assuming any risk.

There's really nothing wrong with being overly safe, but you're going to have a different retirement than someone who assumed a healthy amount of risk while maintaining a sensible portfolio. The low return investments in retirement likely aren't going to afford you the ability to help as many people as you'd like. There may not be much, if anything, left over for your kids. You may have to get on the government roll for some things like healthcare and senior living arrangements, which is also fine, but you need to be aware of that and prepare properly.

Worse than being fearful of financial risk is being fearful of your own success. If you have an entrepreneurial spirit and an idea to make a business work, don't be too afraid to try it. If you are, then you risk losing out on a valuable source of happiness that could last a lifetime.

I took some immense risks to get started, but I took them when I was young, so I had plenty of time and energy to recover from them if I failed. Interestingly enough, that's exactly what happened the first time I tried it—I failed. That's when I picked myself up, dusted myself off, and tried again, because I was young enough, strong enough, and believed in myself enough to make it happen.

Today, I'm very fortunate I had the mental fortitude to start all over again, because I'm financially independent, and I love what I do. The moral of the story is as follows:

don't be afraid to assume some financial or entrepreneurial risk, especially when you're young.

ALL IN THE FAMILY

Let's go back in time to see how I went about assuming that risk early on, the challenges it presented, and how it paid off in the long run.

I met my lovely wife, Julie, while I was obtaining my MBA. It was December, and I had moved to the apartment building where she lived while working as a registered nurse at a nearby hospital. We started dating, and about six months later, my dad's family had a reunion. As you can imagine, a family reunion that involves sixteen kids is quite the spectacle to behold. If I remember correctly, the number of people attending was probably over two hundred.

One of the significant parts of this reunion was an introduction phase, when all the brothers and sisters introduced their kids, grandkids, and so on. When it was time for my dad to introduce his children, he began with my sister and introduced her husband and her kids. Next, it was my turn to be introduced. I was with Julie, whom my dad introduced as my fiancée. Boy, did that get my attention! I started looking at him quizzically, wondering where the heck he was going with such a statement.

After all the introductions were made, people started gathering around Julie and me to congratulate us, and we had to awkwardly explain to everyone that we were just dating. Eventually, the buzz died down, and I was able to catch up to my dad alone.

I said, "Dad, why did you do that? I just met this girl."

He just smiled at me with a twinkle in his bright blue eyes and walked away as if he knew something I didn't. Not even thirty days later, he died.

It's as if he knew Julie would be my wife before I did. His death was one of the most horrible times of my life. He was my everything, and it was extremely hard for me to accept that this wonderful man who pulled me out of an orphanage was now gone.

At the time of my dad's funeral, I barely knew Julie's parents. They came to his service and saw how distraught I was about his passing. So Julie's dad put his arm around me and said, "I'll be your dad now if you want." It was such a generous and compassionate thing to do for someone in need.

Julie and I got engaged in December of that same year, and we were married the following July. We were a young couple just starting out, so these were exciting times.

I graduated with my MBA and was hired by a bank in the nearby town of Hancock, Michigan, which ironically enough is my birth city. Not even one year after we were married, we were expecting our first child and it was time to buy a house. Things were happening fast, and I had a lot to learn as a husband, a father, and a provider.

HOME SWEET HOME

We started by renting our first home, which was a fine option for a young couple just embarking on a new life together. Soon after, we decided to build a brand-new home. Considering our income at the time, this newly built home was a bit of a stretch for our budget. Actually, it was more than just a stretch. It was a burden. Therefore, we needed to remove that two-ton load of long-term debt from our backs, and that's what we did.

It took a long time to sell that home we built. By the time we finally did, we lost most of the equity we put into it. We learned our lesson and moved from Hancock to Marquette, where we purchased a much more reasonably priced home. Sure, it needed a lot of work, and I needed to earn my lost equity dollars back. I did that by putting in an enormous amount of sweat equity.

The little house served us well for a little while. Eventually, it became too small for our growing family to continue living in. So once I earned all that sweat equity back, which took about seven years, we sold it at a nice profit. Then, we were able to move into a colonial on the other side of town, which also needed a little work. But we put some sweat equity in that home as well and stayed there until my youngest child, Ross, graduated from high school. Eventually, we sold that house for a neat profit as well and bought a ranch-style home; perfect for just Julie and me.

The lesson for young people is to rent first. Then, skip the next step I took, which unfortunately was buying a home I couldn't comfortably afford. Instead, if you're at all handy, look at a fixer-upper. If you're there for a long time, that's great, but if it's only a starter home you move on from, that's great too, because the sweat equity you put in will pay off in either scenario.

This is not to say I endorse this for everyone. Of course, it depends on each individual's or couple's circumstances, and the benefits and downside of renting versus owning, which is a personal decision. Ultimately, you should seek the counsel of a qualified financial advisor and/or licensed real estate agent.

My Career Reboot

That time of financial burden from a poor real estate decision was a tough one in our lives, but we made it.

Simultaneously, I was also having some tremendous career struggles, pounding on doors day after day, trying to get people to do business with me.

While my first go-around with entrepreneurship was floundering, our son Ross needed surgery on a double hernia. It wasn't life-threatening, but he needed the surgery nonetheless, and it cost a lot of money. I had a very minimal health insurance policy at the time, so most of the bill was up to us to pay, which we did, but it took just about all the money we had in the bank. There was no financial cushion left for us to fall back on.

At that point, I was like a deer in headlights. The pressure was starting to build, and I was practically begging people to give me their money for investments. Desperation is never a good selling point, however, and I was forced to go back to working at a bank.

The human resources director at my previous bank job called me with an opening for an introductory credit analyst position at a new bank where he worked. It wasn't what I really wanted to do, but it had health insurance, which we recently learned was a critical need. My wife and I both felt it was best for me to take that job.

I ended up working at the bank for the next six years, and it actually worked out very well for me. They eventually made me the manager of the credit department, and I went on to manage the commercial lending department. On the surface, everything seemed great. We were making ends meet, I was fixing up the house, and life was moving along nicely. You might say we were in the non-mindful success space at this time. But I wasn't doing what I wanted to do, and something about that left an emptiness inside me.

Never Give Up!

A chance encounter with a prince of a man from Smith Barney and his wife presented me with an opportunity to get back into financial planning. They wanted me to work for them at their firm, and although I was delighted for the opportunity to fill my career void, I was uncertain if the risk involved with it was the right move for my family. When I told my wife about it, even after the horrible experience we had the first time, she knew it was what I needed to do. Graciously as ever, she said, "All right." I jumped on it, and the rest is history.

That was a very pivotal timeframe in my life and our family's overall well-being. We got through it because we worked hard and stayed together. I've been fortunate for so many things in my life, and it doesn't stop with my parents. My good fortune definitely extends to my beautiful wife. She supported me through all this and had the courage to tell me to go for it when an opportunity to do what I loved presented itself later on. Without her love, strength, and support, who knows what would have happened?

Sometimes, all young people need is a chance. Even if you're having a hard time finding someone to give you that chance, even if you've tried 300 times before, try for number 301. Never give up! Never, ever give up!

Don't Get Caught Up in Today's Must-Have Society

As I look back to when Julie and I were first married and as we raised our kids, we denied ourselves many unnecessary things (wants). We believed strongly in saving and investing for the future, and we, as well as our kids, were better off without all those unnecessary items. Today's must-have society makes it harder than ever to save. You mortgage your future when you buy too much house, take too many trips, or run up the credit cards too high with too many other creature comforts.

Banks might loan you money to buy a lot more house than you should, but I think the old formula for underwriting mortgages is still the best way to approach home buying for young and old alike:

- Twenty percent of the listing price should be used for a down payment.
- Thirty-six percent or less of your gross income should be a debt payment.
- No more than 26 percent of your gross income should go toward your mortgage payment.

It Can Still Be Done

My daughter, Christina, is a great example of how smart saving can still be done, even within the midst of today's must-have society. Coming out of high school, she auditioned for a music scholarship and scored high enough on her ACT to get two scholarships for college. This brought the cost of a private-school education down to the level of a public-school tuition.

Along the way, Julie and I saved some money in a custodial account for her education costs.

These days, there are several choices to help you save for your child's education costs. Current tax law in a 529 college savings program allows all earnings and growth to be distributed for educational costs income tax free.

I also structured my home mortgage to be paid off by the time she started college, so if I needed extra cash flow, I could just take out what I was previously using for the mortgage. We also helped out by buying a car for her.

What kind of car was it, you ask? Was it a brand-new Lexus with heated seats, cruise control, and voice activated navigation? No. It was a used Jeep Cherokee with about 30,000 miles on it, but it was safe, and it got her where she needed to go every day. Since we live in a snow climate, I wanted her to have four-wheel drive. That's why we went with a Jeep.

When she graduated, she was debt free because she had the scholarships and custodial account, and I had some extra cash from some wealth I created to help if she needed it. Many of her friends were leaving college with tremendous debt. They all had big student loans to pay off, which meant they were starting their young, adult lives in debt. What a tough way to start.

Christina took this strategy one step further. She didn't make a lot of money when she first got out of college. Therefore, she underspent on her rent and adjusted her other expenses appropriately to start saving. Eventually, she decided to go back to graduate school and got her master's degree, which she was able to pay for completely on her own. I guess she learned a trick or two from her mom and dad.

Changes in Retirement

So far in this chapter, we've discussed a lot about what it's like to be young and the importance of saving early. Now it's time to discuss the other side of the spectrum—retirement.

Financial planning has always been important, but perhaps even more so now than ever before. Decades ago, you would go to work for a company and they would theoretically take care of you. You could get a job at the phone company or a local manufacturing plant, and they would give you benefits as a reward for your many years of dedicated service and valuable contributions. Health insurance was somewhat affordable, pensions were commonplace, and people could actually count on social security. And let's not forget you could work in the same company for twenty, thirty, or even forty years until you retired. Security and stability existed in the workforce to an extent you don't see anymore.

My father-in-law worked for AT&T for a long time before he retired. He made a very smart move, and as soon as the 401(k) plan was offered, he started investing in it.

Some people are truly blessed because they love what they do and want to do it forever. Others merely show up for work every day and bide their time until they can go home. Even though my father-in-law enjoyed his career, he wanted to move on to the next stage of his life.

I was just coming into the financial advisory business when my father-in-law decided he wanted to retire at the age of fifty-four. I was very young at the time and largely untested in the business, so someone needed to take a chance on me before I could gather some positive momentum. Someone needed to have faith.

Fortunately for me, my father-in-law decided to do just that. He took a chance on me because he trusted me and had faith. We talked about his retirement options, and I advised him to take the lump sum out of his retirement plan rather than the annuity the company offered.

Here is a brief look at all of the options that may exist when deciding how to handle your 401(k) plan with some associated pros and cons:

- Leave money in your former employer's plan, if permitted:
    - Pros: If you like the investments in the plan, you get to stay in them, and you may not incur a fee for leaving it in the plan. This choice does not constitute a taxable event.
- If you weren't retiring but just leaving the company, you could roll over the assets to your new employer's plan, if one is available and it is permitted:
    - Pros: You can keep it all together and have a larger

    sum of money working for you. This also does not constitute a taxable event.
    - Con: Not all employer plans accept rollovers.
- Rollover to an IRA:
    - Pros: You likely have more investment options. It allows for consolidation of accounts and locations. This also does not constitute a taxable event.
    - Cons: There is usually a fee involved. There could also be potential fees for termination.
- Cash out the account:
    - Cons: Cashing out is a taxable event, and there is a potential for loss of investments. This is a costly option for individuals under fifty-nine-and-one-half years of age because it involves a 10 percent penalty in addition to being subject to applicable income taxes.

For additional information and what is suitable for your particular situation, please consult with a reputable financial advisor.

Heeding my advice, my father-in-law trusted me to take his lump sum payment from AT&T and invest it wisely in an IRA. I'm very thankful for his trust, but this was also a wise decision on his part because that lump sum payment evolved into a pool of money that served his family quite well over the last twenty to thirty years. His faith in me served another purpose as well, which was the building of my confidence for which I will always be grateful. Hopefully, the results of investing his money wisely are a thankful payback for his family.

By God's good graces, my investment choices ended up meeting their needs.

Unfortunately, my father-in-law developed Alzheimer's in his early sixties, so he didn't get to enjoy his retirement for very long. The horrible disease ran its course slowly until he passed away at the age of seventy-five, but because those investments fulfilled their needs, my mother-in-law is still doing just fine.

Instead of taking a lump sum, retirees may be able to choose an annuity instead, which is a long-term, tax-deferred insurance contract designed for retirement. Annuities have limitations. If you decide to take your money out early, you may face fees called "surrender charges." Plus, if you're not yet fifty-nine-and-one-half years old, you may also have to pay an additional 10 percent tax penalty on top of ordinary income taxes.

Annuities allow you to create a stream of income through a process called annuitization and may also provide a rate of return based on the terms of the contract. Guarantees and prices are subject to the claims paying ability of the issuing insurance company.

One thing many retirees miss with a fixed annuity is that their purchasing power stays the same over the life of the annuity. Unfortunately, inflation and other economic changes need to be factored in, and twenty years from now, a fixed annuity might not buy what it does today.

The moral of the story is you need to have faith in the future to know your money is going to be there throughout all the ups and downs of the market. Eventually, your investments, as well as your patience and mental fortitude will pay off.

Compliance Note: This case study is for illustrative purposes only. Individual cases will vary. Any information is not a complete summary or statement of all available data necessary for making an investment decision and does not constitute a recommendation. Prior to making any investment decision, you should consult with your financial advisor about your individual financial situation.

People move from one job to another now because they have to. The days of working for the same organization for ten or twenty years are long gone. Companies are in a perpetual state of downsizing and focusing on process improvements rather than creating a lasting corporate culture. It's just the nature of the economic beast these days.

With that in mind, retirement just isn't what it used to

be. For one thing, the cost of living is much higher than it was when my father-in-law retired, but there's much more to it than that. Pensions have all but disappeared. Housing can also be exorbitantly more expensive than it used to be. Healthcare is another cost that's much higher today than it ever was. One hospital stay can be enough to bankrupt someone without decent health insurance.

Compliance Note: For information provided in regard to the story of my father-in-law and I, it should be understood that it is general in nature, is not a complete statement of all information necessary for making an investment decision and is not a recommendation to buy or sell any security or partake in any particular investment strategy. You should consider all your available options and the applicable fees and features of each option before moving your retirement assets.

The Medicare Myth

One thing about retirement that astounds a lot of people is they count on getting Medicare when they reach sixty-five, thinking they're going to have access to free healthcare. What a wonderful world that would be! Unfortunately, it's not so easy.

The problem is, even when you're on Medicare, you're going to have some fairly significant out-of-pocket expenses. Prescription drugs are expensive, and if you're of retirement age, you'll most likely have at least one or two of them you need a constant supply of. That's not to mention routine doctor's exams, procedures, and other minor medical incidents that regularly occur to people of any age. Therefore, you're also going to need a Medigap policy, which again will require premium payments.

Free healthcare in retirement is a myth. In this country, the average person on Medicare can spend a sizable amount on healthcare policies in their retirement years. My clients are flabbergasted when I show them the numbers supporting these facts. Hopefully, when I show them, it's not too late, and they have time to prepare appropriately. By reading this, you've been given even more time to plan.

Life Planning

Retirement and financial planning aren't all about saving. Those are two parts of the bigger picture, which is life planning. Nobody's life plan is the same. We all have different wants, needs, and goals that need to be considered when designing a life plan. Retirement and financial planning need to be considered, but some questions need to be asked first, and a good financial planner will get to know their clients through a discovery process. The Interview Guide we use in our first discovery meeting is shown here:

Total Client Profile Interview Guide

Values

- What's important to you about money?
- What in particular is important to you about that value?
- Is there anything more important than that value?

Goals

- What are your top accomplishments? What would you like them to be?
- What are your personal goals?
- What are your professional goals?
- What do you do (or want to do) for your children?
- What do you do (or want to do) for your parents?
- What do you do (or want to do) for other family members or close friends?
- What do you want to do for the world at large?
- Ideally, where would you like to be when you are forty-five? fifty-five? sixty-five? seventy-five?
- What are your quality-of-life desires (houses, travel, boats, cars)?
- What would you like to achieve with your money?*
- In dollar figures, how much money do you need or want?
- When you think about your money, what concerns, needs, or feelings come to mind?*
- If you didn't have to work anymore, what would you do?

Relationships

- Which family member relationships (spouse, children, siblings, parents, etc.) are the most important ones to you?
- How important are your relationships with people you work with?
- How important are your relationships with people in the community?
- What is your religious orientation? How devout are you? How important are your relationships with people associated with your religion?
- Would you describe yourself as an introvert or an extrovert?
- What pets do you have? How important are they to you?
- What famous people do you know? How did you meet them?
- What schools did you go to? How important is your relationship with these schools?

Assets

- What is your source of income (privately held business, employer, profession)?
- How do you make money today? How is that likely to change in the next three years?
- How do you save or set aside money to invest? How is that likely to change in the next three years?

- What are your investment holdings? Explain your strategy for handling your investments in the way you do.
- What benefits do you get from your workplace?
- What life insurance do you have?
- What property do you have (real property, artwork, jewelry)?
- How are your assets structured now?
- What new assets do you expect to receive (for example, from inheritances or stock options)?
- What is your opinion of taxes? What kinds of taxes bother you the most?
- When you think about your finances, what are your three biggest worries?
- What were your best and worst financial moves? What happened?

Advisors

- Do you have a lawyer? How do you feel about the relationship?
- Do you have a life insurance agent? How do you feel about the relationship?
- Do you have an accountant? How do you feel about the relationship?
- Do you have an investment advisor? How do you feel about the relationship?
- Do you have a financial planner? How do you feel

about the relationship? How frequently have you switched financial planners?

- What were your best and your worst experiences with a professional advisor?
- Of late, how frequently have you switched professional advisors?

Process

- How involved do you like to be in managing your finances?*
- How many face-to-face meetings would you want over the course of a year?
- How often would you like phone updates on your situation?
- Do you want a call about your personal situation when there is a sudden change in the market?
- Do you prefer our written communications to you to be by letter or email?
- What security measures do you want to see used to protect your personal and financial information?
- How often do you want an overall review of your financial situation and progress toward your goals?
- Whom else do you want involved in the management of your finances (spouse, other advisors such as an accountant or an attorney)?
- How important to you is the confidentiality of your financial affairs?*

Interests

- Do you follow sports? Which are your favorite teams?
- What are your favorite types of TV programs and movies?
- What do you read?
- Do you have health concerns or interests? What is your health program?
- Are working out and fitness important to you? What is your program?
- What are your hobbies?
- What would an ideal weekend be?
- What would an ideal vacation be?
- What charitable causes do you donate to? Volunteer for?

*Indicates questions that determine high-net-worth personality.

Source: Prince & Associates

Hypothetically, let's say I have two clients who are both doctors making identical salaries. One of them likes to save, and the other one likes to spend.

For the one who likes to save, it's going to be a fairly easy conversation. We're going to talk a lot about how soon we can make retirement optional. That doesn't mean this doctor has to retire at age sixty-two, sixty-five, or even sixty-seven. That person can work for as long as they want to. In fact, if they get to age sixty-seven and find they still enjoy helping people with their medical knowledge and abilities, that's great. They can keep working if they want to. But what if they enjoy it now, but they don't enjoy it later on when they get older? Or if something makes them physically unable to work at that age, despite a strong will to keep going? In that case, we want to make sure the planning we're doing now is good enough to ensure that option is a reality if and when they need it. It's an optional retirement plan, which is ideal for most people.

For the doctor who likes to spend, that's fine too. It's their life, and they're free to live it the way they want to. But we're going to have a different conversation than we did with the saver. The first thing I'm going to do with this doctor is work out a prioritization schedule because it's important for him to understand the importance of saving and investing for the future. It's going to address some issues like the following:

- Decide the full length of time you want to work. (full time, part time)
- Create a full budget to include where your money is going.
- Separate all expenses into needs, wants, and wishes.
- Identify the realization of the track they're actually on.
- If you own a business, decide your vision for its future (sell it, pass it on to family, etc.)

- Prioritize your life goals.
- Start a realistic plan to make work optional by a certain date.
- Focus on cash flow, tax mitigation, and legacy planning.

From that point, we can start talking about retirement, but we can only do that once we have the facts about their lifestyle and the potentially available pool of money.

A good financial planner will ask questions based on an individual's specific situation. There is no one-size-fits-all life plan, financial plan, or retirement package. It's important to look at life as a whole and understand what needs to be done to get to where you want to be.

Let's use another hypothetical example. This time, we'll discuss someone who doesn't have quite the same income potential as a doctor. For instance, say your son gets out of college at age twenty-two and lands his first real job. However, the benefits don't include a matching 401(k). So it's completely up to him to save appropriately. He starts conservatively by putting $5,000 per year into a Roth IRA, and he intends to do that every year for the next thirty-eight years, until he retires at age sixty.

If we take a look at the industry-standard numbers provided by Ibbotson going back to 1926, stocks have provided a return of 10 to 12 percent. When you're young, you want to invest aggressively, so most of his money, at least in the beginning, should be invested in a diversified portfolio of stocks, but just for the sake of argument, let's say his average rate of return was 8 percent. In thirty-eight years, that young man will have more than $1 million!

It's important to understand that $1 million in thirty-eight years won't buy what it buys today. Much like with the previous example of the annuity, you have to consider inflation. Even after factoring in inflation (for illustrative purposes, call it 2.2 percent), however, that million dollars will be equivalent to around $437,000 in today's dollars? It sounds like a significant decrease, but it's still a sizable amount that can have a large impact on your life.

Also remember, this case involves saving just $5,000 per year. Chances are that fresh out of college, his ability to save is going to grow steadily as his career grows. If he's able to put away $5,000 in year one, he'll likely be able to put away $10,000 by year five, maybe year ten at the most. With this fairly conservative estimate, it's very possible to see someone this financially aware at a young age could have well over $2 million by retirement. That's a nice little nest egg for anybody to draw from.

The Richest Man in Babylon

It doesn't take much to start saving, but unfortunately, one of the things that works against you is that the system works upside down. When you're young, you probably have young kids to feed and clothe, a mortgage payment to make, a car to buy and maintain, and all sorts of other priorities that need to be addressed. What's important is you get started with saving as much as you can possibly afford as soon as you possibly can.

The younger you are when you start planning, the better off you'll be. A good rule of thumb comes from a book that was originally published in 1926. It's called *The Richest Man in Babylon* by George S. Clason. His idea was if you save 10 percent of every dollar you make, you'll be fine later in life and in retirement. Almost one hundred years later, that's still not bad advice. I always tell people to save as much as they can, but if you save at least 10 percent, you're off to a good start.

Reader Notes

At the end of each chapter, there will be a space just like this one where I encourage you to jot down some thoughts or comments of your own, based on what you just read. Hopefully, this book can serve as some sort of inspiration or motivation for your own creativity. From there, maybe your own words will have a positive impact on future generations who pick up the book and hope to learn something from it.

Maybe you'd like to start by making some notes for your own value list? Or maybe there's something else you'd like to share with your son or daughter, or their sons and daughters? Relax, let loose a little, and happy writing!

Chapter Two

Making Wealth Purposeful

Without a rich heart, wealth is an ugly beggar.

—RALPH WALDO EMERSON

Create a passion for what you want to accomplish in life and it will happen. Therefore, if you make purposeful wealth a passion, it's going to happen somehow. Everybody may have a different path to get there, but as long as all those paths are filled with passion, they'll lead to the same road, which will be Wealth Way.

You may have a different idea of purposeful wealth than other people. Purposeful wealth could mean having enough money to help others around you, which reminds me of my dad. He was not a rich man by any stretch of the imagination. My dad wasn't poor either, but he had to work very hard for his money. Something tells me wealth comes much easier for some other people than working twelve-hour days of physical labor between two or more jobs.

One of my dad's biggest principles he lived by was that he was fiercely independent. He had an eighth-grade education, but he always found a way to pay for everything his family needed while taking care of all the building maintenance around the house and his motel business on his own (with a lot of after-school help from me).

Through this fiercely independent spirit, my father created his own form of purposeful wealth. He was completely opposed to charging anyone a nickel over what he thought was a fair price for one of his motel rooms. I distinctly remember my mother and him charging people $8.48 per night to stay in one of those cabins. In his mind, he would rather work harder for his whole life than have to charge anything more than what he thought was fair for one of those rooms.

Know Your Goals and Values

As a financial advisor, I get to help people discover what their own version of purposeful wealth is. The first meeting I have with a client is called a discovery meeting. It's a process in which I get to know them a little better. You may find yourself in a meeting with a financial advisor who doesn't take this time to discover who you are and what your values might be. They may just cram your life savings into a one-size-fits-all financial product, pat you on the back, and whisk you out the door. I would say you deserve better than that.

The discovery process of knowing your values should help a good financial advisor to determine if your hopes and dreams align congruently with your financial situation. Sometimes, I have very difficult discussions with people because their hopes and dreams don't line up with their available resources. At that point, we would need to discuss alternatives that may get them going in an optimistic direction rather than feeling any form of despair or hopelessness. Again, consider the base discovery questions we go over in our initial meeting as previously illustrated.

Aha!

A fairly typical scenario in my office is a husband and wife who are near retirement age—mid to late fifties—and they realize they want to retire, but never had any clear purpose for their wealth. That's not a matter of right or wrong. They've been living their life together and didn't have wealth creation as a goal, but now, they want to figure out how they can make retirement happen, which may be easier said than done at this point.

The discovery process teaches me a lot about these clients. From there, I'm able to create a financial roadmap for them. We usually map out a retirement plan for around thirty years. Here's some of the questions we ask in the discovery meeting that's going to help us design an effective plan.

- What is important to you about money?
- What are your personal goals for your money?
- When you think about money, what concerns, needs, and feelings come to you mind?
- What do you want for your kids?
- Do you have living parents who might need care now or some day in the future?

At that point of the discovery process, they might look at each other and start to panic a little. They may even say something like, "We never thought about any of that stuff. We're going to work until the day we die, aren't we?"

That's when I need to calm them down and make them understand we're going to come up with a plan for them. It may not be ideal in their minds, but it's going to be a plan they can act on immediately and take some solace in.

The first thing we do is prioritize things in their life. Then, I gather all their financial data to start a customized plan for them.

By the time they leave my office, couples like that usually feel a little better about their financial awareness. They have an aha moment and feel as if they understand how to make retirement work a lot more.

One of our missions—as financial advisors—is to have a big impact on our clients' overall well-being. If we can provide someone with guidance that awakens them to a financial reality, that's a tremendously gratifying feeling for us.

Around seven to ten business days will elapse before our next session with that couple, which is a planning meeting. This is when most people have a second aha moment. We start this meeting by presenting them with an assumptive Monte Carlo analysis. We also separate basic retirement expenses such as automobiles, daily living, a second home purchase, college expenses, travel, and healthcare, etc.

Almost everybody hates separating these expenses and accounting them, but it's necessary to really develop a good plan that actually means something. Different dynamics go into this process. Expenses change and plans change, so the plan needs to be adjusted, but we need to have a foundation to begin with. It's all part of a financial awakening I think is necessary for them to truly understand the reasoning behind our plan.

Steering the Ship

From that budget and the declaration of their goals and objectives, we'll design a plan that dictates what they'll have to live on if they retire at age sixty-two, sixty-five, sixty-seven, or whatever age they desire.

We'll structure the portfolio to reach their stated goals. An important factor in portfolio design is their legacy goals. Do they want to maintain their principle balance, grow it, or use it by a certain age?

I've had a few clients tell me at the beginning of our relationship they would like to spend their last dime on the day they die. However, when their portfolio starts to decrease in value during short-term market drops, they become uncomfortable and realize they want to at least maintain their current values. Therefore, after we run a Monte Carlo simulation for them with all expected expenses, resources or income, and their financial assets they'll have a good idea how things may work out. From this Monte Carlo analysis, we'll create a personal financial policy statement.

This document will put us all on the same page...no surprises. This is just the first step. Going forward we'll need to review all life data and follow their plan. In some cases, we'll make adjustments. This ship has set sail and now needs a captain to guide it along.

By the time they leave our office with a plan, at least they have a direction going forward. Somebody once said if you put a ship in the ocean with no captain, it could end up on any shore. I think that's true, which is why I love what I do so much. I can help people steer their boat to exactly the shore they want to be on.

Wise Decisions

Steering the ship for retirement is one very important aspect of what I do as a financial advisor. However, the sooner someone can steer that ship in the right direction, the better for your long-term wealth management. Therefore, making wise decisions before your mid to late fifties is optimal.

Naively, some clients will come to my office with—as an example—$800,000 in cash and bonds for their retirement savings they want to reallocate into a more diversified strategy. It's a wise decision, but unfortunately, one they probably should have made a long time ago. Although cash and bonds are generally stable, they're not going to grow wealth at the rate a long-term diversified equity portfolio will. Cash and bonds are a fine option, but diversification with stocks and other investments will have much more favorable results, which we'll discuss in greater detail in Chapter 5.

FIVE BAGS OF GOLD

Matthew 25:14–30 (New International Version) is known as "The Parable of the Five Bags of Gold." It's a long text with some excellent insight into the most vulnerable and potentially crippling of human emotions, which is fear. The added relevance of that story for our purpose is it concerns fear in relation to gold, which we can easily translate into modern language as money.

> This biblical story starts with a master who is going on a long journey. Before he leaves, he entrusts his wealth to his servants. The master gives five bags of gold to one particularly wise and capable servant, two bags to another, and only one bag to a third servant.
>
> The servant who was entrusted with five bags of gold put the money to work immediately and doubled the wealth. His master replied, "Well done, good and faithful servant! You have been faithful with a few things; I will put you in charge of many things."
>
> The servant who was given two bags of gold also put the money to work and doubled the wealth. His master responded with a similar sentiment of satisfaction and reward.
>
> The third servant who was given only one bag of gold, however, did not put the money to work. Instead, he

> dug a hole in the ground and buried the money. He was fearful of losing the money his master worked so hard for, so he hid it to ensure none of it would be lost when his master returned. When his master returned, he scolded the third servant for his actions by exclaiming, "You wicked, lazy servant! So, you knew that I harvest where I have not sown and gather where I have not scattered seed? You should have put my money on deposit with the bankers, so that when I returned I would have received it back with interest. So, take the bag of gold from him and give it to the one who has ten bags. For whoever has will be given more, and they will have an abundance. Whoever does not have, even what they have will be taken from them. And throw that worthless servant outside, into the darkness, where there will be weeping and gnashing of teeth."

Fear is at the essence of this parable. The servants who weren't fearful were marvelously successful in doubling their wealth. With this story, the Bible teaches us that fear comes from a lack of faith. The servant who was cast in the darkness is probably a good-hearted soul, but he lacked faith. He was crippled with fear, so he didn't even play it safe by banking the money to get a miniscule interest rate in return. Instead, he just buried it, and the Lord pointed out his misdeed for all his children to learn from. Much of this story is written in red, which means the words are coming directly from Jesus. Therefore, it seems Jesus is using this story to teach us not to be afraid, but to act wisely, have strong faith, and live without fear, for it has a paralyzing potential.

I can't tell my clients not to worry, but maybe the Lord will profess this lesson to them through their own faith. The best thing I can do is lead by example. I can show my clients, my children, and the children of my clients how I live, and hopefully that helps them to live through faith, rather than fear. St. Francis of Assisi once said, "Go forth into the world, and preach and evangelize for Jesus Christ. Only use words when you have to." He's telling us to live by example, which I firmly believe is a noble and worthy cause.

Life Is a Stock, Not a Bond

Bonds have a slow, steady crawl to maturity. That's not what life is like. Only for a short period of time do we crawl as babies before we walk. After that, it's a matter of days before we're happy-go-lucky toddlers running as fast as our God-given little legs will take us to chase the family dog in the backyard. Stocks, however, are up and down. That's what life is. Life has some beautiful ups, but it also has some very challenging downs. If you can accept that certainty, you can live a much richer life, free from fear.

Your financial wealth will act similarly to your life—there

will be ups and downs over a long period of time. You need to have some purpose for creating wealth that will provide a steady course to follow while you're riding those ups and downs of your financial life. That's the biggest reason to find a smart financial advisor, one who understands good financial planning is about more than cramming your life savings into a one-size-fits-all portfolio. You want a person you can confide your goals to, and the purpose for your wealth creation, so they can customize a plan that will provide that steady course for your particular lifestyle.

Reader Notes

This chapter discussed the idea of purposeful wealth. I encourage you to write down some notes to your children here about this very important aspect of your life planning.

Chapter Three

Choosing the Right Advisor

Those who won't be counseled, can't be helped.

—BENJAMIN FRANKLIN

The financial crisis of 2008 is considered to be the worst of its kind since the Great Depression of the 1930s. It was a bear market that lasted from October 2007 to March 2009. During that time, the Dow Jones Industrial Average (DJIA) plunged a total of 54 percent. Spawned largely by unethical practices in the subprime mortgage market, banks that were deemed too big to fail...failed. If there was a big, red panic button on the front lawn of the White House, there likely would have been a steady stream of panicked politicians and devastated investors rushing to push it.

Some people called us after the calamity, saying they

sold out their stock positions during the market storm and put their investments in bonds and cash, which of course was a big mistake.

Guess what happened after March 2009? A bull market took over. Thanks to cooler heads, some serious governmental interventions, and wise decision-making, the market recovered, as it always has in the past.

Choose Strength

A good financial advisor should remove emotion from the equation and be strong enough to know not to panic. Fear has a trickle-down effect from the media to the advisor to the individual investor. Once fear spreads, it's like a sickness, and only the strong will survive. If your advisor allows fear to consume their decision-making, you're going to suffer for it.

For example, if you sold at the bottom of that market—in March of 2009—when the DJIA dropped to approximately 6,500, it repaired and not only crossed the previous high (in the fall of 2007) of 14,200, but it is now over 24,000—hard to believe. I can think of a few clients off the top of my head who came to us after they moved at the bottom of that bear market, and we've helped them, but by their previous mistake of selling out, a good portion of their wealth will never be recovered.

Nostradamus (Fortune-Tellers) Need Not Apply

Yes, financial advisors need to be strong, and they need to remove emotion from the equation. However, do they need to be able to predict the future? Absolutely not. In fact, if you find yourself in a meeting with one who claims they can, run—don't walk—out of their office as fast as you can because your hard-earned money is not in a good place there. Financial advisors do not time the market or make predictions because they're not soothsayers. They're just the opposite. All they do is make sound decisions based on historical performance, current facts, and individual client needs.

I expect you, as a client, to act out of fear a lot of the time because there's a lot at stake and you probably don't have the background to understand how the market works. If you see a downward trend, you might try to lure your financial advisor into giving you the okay to get out of your beautifully structured strategic portfolio. If they tell you okay, then you might assume they'll tell you when to get back in. The truth is, nobody knows when to get back in. The best course of action is to just hold steady, and once the market comes back, you'll reap the rewards of your patience. Whereas, if you sell low and then wait too long to get back in, you may have missed out on 10, 20, or 30 percent or more in return.

Instead of trying to be Nostradamus, a good financial

advisor should be fully engaged in planning and structuring investments according to our three main investment principles, which are asset allocation, diversification, and annual rebalancing. In return, we ask our clients to abide by a different three principles, which are trust, patience, and discipline. Together, these two groups of principles form our Six Guiding Principles of Investing at our firm.

Strategic Diversification Is Key

Rather than trying to look into a crystal ball, read your palms, or predict the future in any other mystical and fraudulent fashion, a good advisor will wisely direct you to strategic diversification. For example, if you come to me with the desire to make retirement happen within the next year, after a thorough discovery analysis, we'll create a healthy (diversified) mixture of stocks, bonds, and cash. If your withdrawal rate from that portfolio is an average of 4 percent, that means I'll put a minimum of 30 to 40 percent in bonds. The remainder should achieve net growth to protect purchasing power.

Specific investments get strategically driven from that overarching strategy. We put a certain amount in large capitalization growth, large capitalization value, small capitalization growth, and small capitalization value. Then, we'll have some in developed international, emerging markets, and a small piece in either real estate or a group of commodities.

At the end of the year and annually thereafter, we'll rebalance that portfolio to ensure all of your bases are still covered. Financial investing is not a one-shot deal. The advisor you choose should work closely with you on an ongoing basis for security and wealth.

By investing in a wise balance of funds, you achieve a diversified portfolio, no matter what the size of your egg is. You've covered all bases at that point, and you're not gambling on any of them. If gambling is your thing, go to Las Vegas and play your game of choice, but choose a good financial advisor for smart goal-based financial planning and more importantly, financial behavior consulting.

Weathering the Storm

Every so often, crisis inevitably hits. It's not a prediction. It's not a foreshadowing. It's not even a moderately bold statement. It's a fact of life. Google this quick query: "financial crisis." You'll see they date back to the first century.

In the year AD 33 historians claim a crisis hit the Roman Empire when there was a mass issuance of unsecured loans by banking houses. In more modern times, the

United States has seen several economic eras flawed by crisis, such as the Great Depression of the 1930s, the recession of the 1980s, the dot-com bubble of the early 2000s, and the subprime mortgage crisis of 2008. If you take nothing else from this book, heed the following advice: stay strong and weather the storm because, so far, there has never been a permanent market drop.

Pointing out those financial meltdowns isn't meant to make you stuff all your money in the mattress and build a bomb shelter. You don't need to hide until a new world of financial equality somehow forms amid the chaos of political unrest. Far from it, I just want you to realize financial crises happen, but good financial advisors can help you weather the storm.

Let's say you have a typical 60/40 portfolio of stocks and bonds. When you draw money from it for your living expenses, consider drawing from bonds, but not stocks. Once per year, my firm will perform a rebalancing back into stocks. This rebalancing may be delayed if stocks are down in value, but since we have a detailed personal financial policy statement, when we go to rebalance, very little will be done, for the withdrawals have lowered the bond values, and (in this example) stock values are also down. Let's say the stocks have recovered the next year. Now, a meaningful rebalance will occur. By the way, this is why we will typically keep

30 to 40 percent in short to intermediate bonds. We generally have four to six years' worth of withdrawals available in the bond portfolio. This should remove a lot of the stock market risk for a retiree drawing from their portfolio. That way, you don't risk ravaging your portfolio. Instead, you're allocating investments on a periodic basis to adjust for changes in the market and your own lifestyle.

No matter how smart you are at diversifying your money, market trouble is going to happen, and it's going to seem scary for a little while. Stay strong because you should have plenty of money on the bond side of your portfolio, which should provide a stable pool of money to draw from. If the stock market declines for a period of time, you should not be negatively affected.

A well-designed bond allocation in an overall retirement portfolio should be non-correlated to stocks. This acts as a very low volatility portion of your savings. The bond allocation is generally a much more level performing investment option.

In my opinion, bonds are generally not a good long-term investment, but when you're retired and withdrawing from your portfolio, it only makes sense to have some amount safely invested in them. That way, when you see the storm coming, and you think you're exacerbating the problem by drawing money during retirement, you can relax knowing two things:

1. You're only drawing from bonds, where the values may not change much in a bear market.
2. When the equity markets repair—typically within one to two years—the bonds will be replenished from the stocks back to the desired strategy in the personal financial policy statement.

Compliance Note: Diversification and asset allocation do not ensure a profit or protect against a loss. Past performance is not indicative of future results. Investing always involves risk, and you may incur a profit or loss. Holding stocks for the long term does not ensure a profitable outcome. Investing in stocks always involves risk, including the possibility of losing one's entire investment.

Sector investments are companies engaged in business related to a specific sector. They are subject to fierce competition, and their products and services may be subject to rapid obsolescence. There are additional risks associated with investing in an individual sector, including limited diversification.

International investing involves special risks, including currency fluctuations, differing financial accounting standards, and possible political and economic volatility.

Investing in emerging markets can be risker than investing in well-established foreign markets.

Commodities investing is generally considered speculative because of the significant potential for investment loss. Their markets are likely to be volatile, and there may be sharp price fluctuations even during periods when prices overall are rising.

Rebalancing a non-retirement account could be a taxable event that may increase your tax liability. No investment strategy can guarantee success.

Three Foundational Criteria for the Right Advisor

There are three components of any good working relationship. It doesn't matter if you're seeking a doctor, a lawyer, or a financial advisor. If trust, competence, and good rapport are at the heart of the relationship, it will be a productive one.

It's a Matter of Trust

The most important thing we ask of our clients in my financial group is to trust us. My recommendation to all our clients is for them to meet with at least three different financial advisors before choosing one. Nothing establishes trust better than giving people the freedom to talk to others vying for the same business.

Not so long ago, a young man walked into our office seeking financial advice. One of my advisors pulled me out of a meeting, and said, "I think you should come talk to this gentleman."

Normally, I focus on clients with high net worth, but I also shepherd the rest of the clients in my firm and watch over the whole business. This young man was very impressive in his demeanor, attitude, and his desire to do the right thing. I got to know him quite well through our interactions and quickly discovered he was also a hardworking family man with a demanding job as a manager at a local retail store. He came to us looking for some advice about a recent financial situation he found himself in.

This fine young man had a three-year-old daughter and a pregnant wife, whom he had recently taken to the hospital because of some medical issues. Tragically, her situation worsened soon after they arrived, and neither she, nor her unborn son made it.

Now, this young man found himself with the extremely challenging task of carrying on without his wife while also caring for his young daughter, who must now face life without her mother. It's an awful situation for anyone to be in, and it only got more complicated from the ensuing court case that followed.

Some financial damages were justly awarded to the young man and his daughter. Unfortunately, the attorneys also got a disproportionately large chunk of the money, which is just the way the world works.

This young man received only $100,000, while the attorneys received $500,000 for their efforts. Fortunately, the three-year-old daughter did receive $400,000, which was the reason he was coming to see us. The attorneys did their job and were now finished. They did suggest an annuity to the father, which may have been a good alternative. However, while annuities may be appropriate depending upon an individual's situation, I'm not a big fan of them because I've seen the client get the short end of the stick many times.

I talked with this young man for quite a while and got as much information as I could about what he wanted for a long-term objective for the money. We put together a financial plan and a personal financial policy. I told him I would invest his money as if it were my daughter's future on the line, and I explained how we would do it. Finally, I told him not to rush into anything with us. I wanted him to talk to two more financial advisors before he made any decisions.

The young man took my advice to heart, met with two more advisors, and came back a couple weeks later. He said, "I definitely want to work with you guys." From there, we not only helped the young man with a sound financial plan, but we also instilled a trust factor with him.

It struck him as odd that we actually wanted him to talk to our competitors, but it made him feel free. The normal human reaction when you want something is to grip it very tightly, but the best relationships are always the ones with freedom in them because freedom establishes trust, and trust is invaluable.

Compliance Note: This case study is for illustrative purposes only. Individual cases will vary. Any information is not a complete summary or statement of all available data necessary for making an investment decision and does not constitute a recommendation. Prior to making any investment decision, you should consult with your financial advisor about your individual situation.

Openness, freedom, and trust are three key factors when selecting a financial advisor. Another thing to look for is some key designations of academic excellence. Of course, years of experience from a seasoned financial advisor are also invaluable.

Evaluating Competence

A strong academic background goes a long way in exemplifying competence. There are three educational components I have found tremendously helpful in my career. I have earned my MBA, am a Certified Financial Planner (CFP®), and am a Certified Investment Management Analyst (CIMA®). Obtaining these degrees doesn't necessarily guarantee competence in a financial advisor, but I can personally vouch for the amount of work required and the high standards involved in getting them, which definitely counts for something.

Compliance Note: Certified Financial Planner Board of Standards Inc. owns the certification marks CFP®, CERTIFIED FINANCIAL PLANNER™, and federally registered CFP® (with flame design) in the US, which it awards to individuals who successfully complete CFP® Board's initial and ongoing certification requirements.

My MBA from Northern Michigan University was phenomenally effective in teaching me the four big disciplines of accounting, economics, marketing, and finance. Of course, I focused on the finance part of that instruction, but I acquired a very well-rounded background in the other three areas from my degree as well. The MBA has enabled me to give my clients a wealth of knowledge, many decades past my commencement date, based on all four disciplines.

Many of my clients are business owners. My experience growing up with my parents' business, as well as my own entrepreneurial endeavors and commercial banking background has given me a perspective to help them with their marketing, balance sheets, P&Ls, and many other issues they're facing.

The scope of learning in the CFP® is miles wide and an inch deep. It taught me all about how to be the quarterback for a client's life plan. The CFP® program is focused on protection, accumulation, distribution, and legacy. It's what prepares you to assist an individual with determining the needs of their entire financial situation. You learn how to work with a client through all four phases of their financial life.

My Certified Investment Management Analyst (CIMA®) designation was issued by the Investments and Wealth Institute, which is an esteemed group in the financial world. I attended the program through The Wharton Business School at the University of Pennsylvania, which focused on wealth management for individuals, businesses, and institutions. That is a much more granular course of study with a lot of technical knowledge and mathematics involved. It teaches the science of building portfolios, managing money, and metrics such as alpha, beta, standard deviations, sharp ratios, R^2, etc.

Competence extends far beyond the academic world.

Keep in mind, both the A and the C student pass most of those exams, and you may not necessarily want the C student planning your financial future. That's why you need to use your best judgement and your own eye for discernment when evaluating a financial advisor.

The planner you choose should have an iron-clad process. If they start by recommending investments before they get to know you and what your goals are, that's a big, blazing-hot, red flag. This means they're either making it up as they go along, or they just cram every client they meet into a one-size-fits-all financial plan, neither of which are any good.

Establishing Rapport

When you walk into the office of a doctor, an accountant's, or a financial planner, you likely feel an aura right away. I'm not trying to be too mystical or new age by mentioning this, but I feel like most of us get a vibe—either good or bad—as soon as we walk into a new situation. If you get a bad vibe as soon as you meet someone, you will need to dig deep into your discernment barrel. If you get a good vibe, however, you will know there's something more to consider there.

Establishing good rapport goes beyond the first impression. Both parties should enjoy their time together at least a little. You don't need to look forward to meeting with your financial advisor the same way you would look forward to Christmas when you were a child, but you shouldn't dread seeing them. If you wake up in the morning and immediately feel awful because you have a meeting with your financial advisor that day, and you know they're going to ask you a bunch of uncomfortable questions, you should probably take your business elsewhere.

That's why we always try to get to know our clients on a deeper level at my firm. Our initial discovery meeting we have is so important because it tells us a lot about your personal side as well as your goals and objectives. We get to hear about how many kids you have, what grades they're in, and what they're doing so far in life. There's more we'll find out about your passions, hobbies, and social engagements. Not only does all this information help us plan your finances, but it also establishes a very valuable rapport. We get to know you, and whenever you come in for a six-month or annual meeting, we'll ask you how your kids are doing and how you enjoyed the cruise you went on for your twenty-fifth anniversary. We like to understand what your successes were since we last spoke and what we need to focus on for the next six months. It becomes a personal matter that people value, which is a good thing.

Measuring everything by the horizon can get frustrating. Sometimes, you need to step back and recognize what you've accomplished over the last month or two to maintain a healthy and positive mindset. After you can appreciate some of your more short-term accomplishments, you become more attuned with your more far-reaching goals and longer objectives.

Good Advice Costs...Something

Good advice might cost less than you think. It's not free; it does cost something. Free always sounds good, but it rarely—if ever—produces good results.

Once you have a firm understanding of what an experienced, knowledgeable financial advisor can do, you'll discover they're well worth what they charge. For example, let's say you pay someone 1 percent to manage your financial assets, or more accurately, your financial behavior. What if they save you 5 to 6 percent in market-timing mistakes. In that fairly typical scenario, their services prove to be well worth the fee.

When choosing the right advisor, you may see some firms charging as high as 3 percent, which is fine, but the industry average is currently less. That fee has come down over the years for a few reasons.

Compliance Note: In a fee-based account, clients pay a

quarterly fee based on the level of assets in the account for the services of a financial advisor as part of an advisory relationship. In deciding to pay a fee rather than commissions, clients should understand the fee may be higher than a commission alternative during periods of lower trading.

Advisory fees are in addition to the internal expenses charged by mutual funds and other investment company securities. To the extent that clients intend to hold these securities, the internal expenses should be included when evaluating the costs of a fee-based account.

Clients should periodically reevaluate whether the use of an asset-based fee continues to be appropriate in servicing their needs. A list of additional considerations, as well as the fee schedule, is available in the firm's Form ADV Part 2A, as well as the client agreement.

Some are giving credence to robo-advisors. They may have a valid role; however, it is very limited. Robo-advisors look strictly at asset allocation of investment, and the firms that use them charge very little for that service. However, if you want real advice from a human perspective, it's going to cost a little more. A robo-advisor can't look at behavioral aspects and accurately determine which funds and institutional managers will comprise the best portfolio based on your individual needs. They're also not going to have the strength it takes to stop you from making a big mistake, like selling low in a bear market. Is that worth 1 percent? I say it's worth far more, but 1 percent is a good target when smartly choosing an advisor.

The Role of Faith in Choosing a Financial Advisor

Choosing a financial advisor requires faith more than anything. Your role as an investor is to use your best judgement of competence in your choice, establish a rapport, and trust your advisor. Trust is built on the foundation of faith. Miracles have happened when faith was at the heart of a relationship or situation. Let's examine a couple more biblical verses for some evidence.

There may be no better shining example of faith than what lies within the heart of Mary, the mother of Jesus. When the angel Gabriel approached her about becoming the mother of Jesus Christ, she calmly and faithfully replied, "To me, be it done." Despite the fact she was risking being shunned and divorced by Joseph, whom she was betrothed to, she had such a wealth of faith, she was able to accept her role and serve God.

Where there is no faith, no miracles happen. This is evident in the story of Jesus revisiting his hometown I mentioned earlier. Very few, if any miracles happened during that time because the people had no faith. Actually, they pretty much threw him out of town.

Transferring the idea of biblical faith to the current world and financial planning, we may not be able to perform miracles, but we can still do a lot of good. Consider the following quote from a man who is known more for his scientific genius than economic wisdom, but it's very poignant for our discussion.

Albert Einstein once said, "Compounded interest is the eighth wonder of the world. He who understands it, earns it...he who doesn't...pays it."

Through Einstein's interpretation of the eighth wonder of the world, we can provide some clients with the illusion of a miracle. One client of mine who was an AT&T retiree, had around $300,000 to work with. After we performed his review several years later, we realized he withdrew about $300,000, but now his account was still at $350,000. After opening his eyes to this revelation, he said, "So I started with $300,000. I took out over $300,000, and I'm still left with $350,000? How the heck did that happen? That's a miracle!"

Another client came to me many years ago, and we rode through the economic storms of 2000 and 2008 together. He was about to retire, and he had a decent amount of money saved, but it was all in one-year CDs. I ran the numbers to show him the direction his current plan was taking him, and he was not going to be able to make it work. So I restructured his portfolio into a healthy mix of stocks and bonds based on his personal situation.

Then came the dot-com crash of 2000 and a near economic collapse in 2008. During that last storm, he said to me, "Mark, I can't go back to work because I'm too old. But I'm scared. You have all my money. What should I do?"

I told him, "I know this is tough for you and your wife, but you'll get through this, and you're going to be just fine." I went on to give him the same advice I gave everybody during those times, which is to stay strong because the market will recover.

At the time, he was around seventy-five years old and drawing from his account for living expenses, which is what he's still doing today. After all that turmoil and withdrawing 4 to 5 percent out per year, he still has more than when he started his retirement.

Maybe we can work miracles...

Compliance Note: Case studies are for illustrative purposes only. Individual cases will vary. Any information is not a complete summary or statement of all available data necessary for making an investment decision and does not constitute a recommendation. Prior to making any investment decision, you should consult with your financial advisor about your individual situation.

Reader Notes

Write down notes to your children (or other loved ones) about the importance of working with a financial advisor.

Chapter Four

Creating Wealth

In short, the way to wealth, if you desire, it is as plain as the way to market. It depends chiefly on two words—industry and frugality. That is, waste neither time nor money, but make the best use of both.

—BENJAMIN FRANKLIN

The preceding quote from one of the founding fathers of our country—his second in this book—is a little dated because he talks about "the way to market," but what holds up is the overall meaning of the quote, which is the importance of industry and frugality in creating wealth. A more simplistic, but not nearly as poetic, way of saying this is "We should be industrious with our God-given talents and spend less than what we earn."

Frugality + Industriousness = Wealth Creation

There's really no other way to do it, other than just luck.

You could win the lottery.

You could inherit a fortune from a rich uncle.

And maybe a plane full of one-hundred-dollar bills will fly over your house one day and just drop its entire cargo for your benefit.

Truth is, none of those things are very likely to happen. From what I've read about the odds of winning the lottery, your chances might be better with the plane situation.

INDUSTRIOUSNESS

The first aspect of that equation is industriousness, which requires a bit of context to fully comprehend. Bill Gates, Steve Jobs, Warren Buffet, and Benjamin Graham are all people who used their God-given talents to create immense wealth. In other words, they were or are industrious.

Bill Gates used his talents as a programmer and a businessman to create Microsoft.

Steve Jobs created Apple with a remarkably clear vision and a unique ability to innovate.

Warren Buffet is one of the most successful investors in the history of the world.

And Benjamin Graham is considered the father of value investing. He was also a brilliant economist, an esteemed professor, as well as the creator of the model by which Buffet gained so much of his success.

Chances are, you're not going to be able to create as much wealth as those giants of industry. Not only are their talents remarkably special, but they also had a few things break their way to achieve the level of success most will only dream of.

However, you can still be industrious in your own little world. If you have a job working for a big corporation, you can do that job to the best of your God-given ability for that corporation. Just by having an awareness to excel at whatever you do will likely move you up the chain of command and create more wealth.

If it's within your genetic makeup to forge your own path, make your own decisions, and use your own creativity, then you can be industrious as a freelancer or an entrepreneur, which although a bit riskier, has a much higher ceiling for the wealth you can create.

Frugality is the simplest aspect of wealth creation; just

spend less and save more. If you can save 10 percent of your income, whether it's 10 percent of $50,000 or 10 percent of $500,000, you'll have achieved a sufficient level of frugality to create wealth.

My dad was a great example of how you can be industrious and frugal while knowing next to nothing about finance. At one point, he had eleven paychecks stacked up without cashing them. That was his idea of saving. He worked extremely hard between his job at the mine and the cabins he owned with my mother, but he was also one of the most frugal guys I've ever known.

Perspective

You don't need to be Warren Buffett to create substantial wealth for your own personal situation. Think about a young couple just getting out of college and beginning their careers. By dollar cost averaging over their lifetime, they will see many ups and downs in the stock market. However, when they get ready to retire, do you think they will be better off for saving money?

Compliance Note: Dollar-cost averaging cannot guarantee a profit or protect against a loss, and you should consider your financial ability to continue purchases through periods of low price levels.

Truth or Consequences

Now that you have the proper perspective of what wealth creation can look like for you, it's important to understand how the decisions we make influence our financial future.

The past is what holds all our memories. It can be a source of great joy, but it can also be a source of tremendous pain. The key is not to live there. If you can hold on to the good memories, and get over the bad ones, the past can be like a long-lost friend. It's also crucial to accept an appropriate level of responsibility.

The present is the moment we live in. If you don't live in the moment, you risk missing out on so much beauty. It's very important to not dwell in the past so you don't miss what's happening right before your eyes. If you're filled with regret or constantly fretting over what has happened or what may happen, you will miss the true value in the world around you.

The future is where your trusted financial advisor can help to create wealth. The whole idea of wealth creation is to enable a successful future. You, the investor, don't need to live in the future. That's what we do. We strive to create a roadmap to help people get to where they want to be in the future based on their current circumstances and areas of need.

Occasionally, I need to make some of my clients face a truth with which they may not be comfortable. After I get a full understanding of their situation in life, I may have to tell them the roadmap they're currently using isn't going to get them where they want to be in retirement. They're about to encounter the consequences for the decisions they've made up to this point.

The decisions that have led most people to a future they hadn't envisioned as ideal usually has to do with a lack of either industriousness or frugality. None of this means these people had any ill intent or any selfishness. Things may have just not lined up for them the way they wanted. Maybe the career they chose, even though it was fulfilling emotionally, wasn't financially stable. In that case, they may be very rich in spirit, but unfortunately, retirement could be difficult for them.

Others may have had a difficult time with the frugality side of the equation. Maybe they valued current comfort over future well-being, which is also a fine way to live, but your future may suffer as a consequence of that decision.

The Basic Building Blocks of a Strong Portfolio

If you are properly industrious and frugal, and you make

the wise decision to save for the future, the next thing you need to think about is building a strong financial portfolio.

What does a strong portfolio look like? In short, simplicity is the key once again. A large portion of the financial industry today is making things unnecessarily complicated with new products the average investor doesn't need to understand. Hedge funds, long strategies, short strategies, and other overly complex mutual funds are confusing people. You don't need to know about any of it.

I've been in this business for a long time, and I've seen a lot of different strategies and approaches. Any time I hear of anything new, I always say, "If you can tell me where this isn't going to cost more and the long-term return isn't any less than your current strategy, then I'm all ears." The problem is it always costs more, and the return is usually less as well.

The basic building blocks of a strong portfolio that creates wealth steadily over a reasonable period of time are the same they've been for many decades, which are the ownership of great businesses around the globe, as well as ownership of real estate. Complete portfolio management, however, may include cash and bonds. Don't just take my word for it either. The historical data backs it up.

This graphic is a time-tested, proven statistical indicator

of how investments have performed from 1926–2016. It's a continuing system that's constantly updated and models the previous time periods. The Ibbotson chart depicted here isolates each of the basic building blocks I mentioned, as well as some other investment choices.

Stocks, Bond, Bills, and Inflation: 1926–2016

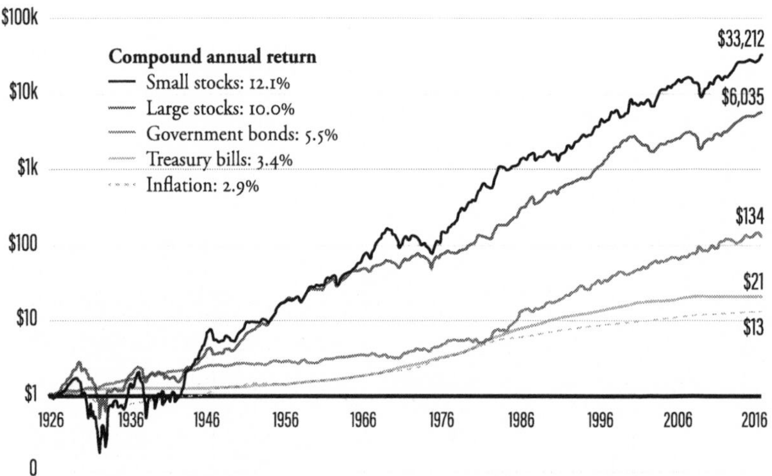

Past performance is no guarantee of future results. Hypothetical value of $1 invested at the beginning of 1926. Assumes reinvestment of income and no transaction costs or taxes. This is for illustrative purposes only and not indicative of any investment. An investment cannot be made directly in an index.

Mutual Funds

Mutual funds can be stocks, bonds, or cash. It is a professionally managed investment program that provides diversification for small investors. They can be a good mixture of all the building blocks for the average investor who otherwise wouldn't have the necessary resources to get good diversification.

Your financial advisor can select good mutual funds by picking those that are managed well and making sure the portfolio aligns with your investment objectives. We look at specific investment styles and measure the risk versus reward. We'll also look at peer group rankings and compare active to passive strategies.

Exchange-Traded Funds (ETFs)

Exchange traded funds are gaining in popularity. To provide you with a textbook definition from Investopedia, An ETF is "a marketable security that tracks an index, a commodity, bonds, or a basket of assets like an index fund. Unlike mutual funds, an **ETF** trades like a common stock on a stock exchange. ETFs experience price changes throughout the day as they are bought and sold."

Individual Stocks

If you have an individual stock you want to invest in, you should do it. People have had great success in the past just investing in a stock they truly believe in. It's also very satisfying when you believe in something strongly enough to take a chance on it and it pays off for you.

It might be a specific technology you think is going to be a game changer.

It might be a company you have an earnest belief in how they operate.

It might be a product you've just always felt good about or have a high opinion of.

This book isn't meant to serve as an in-depth explanation of various investments, so I'm only going to mention certain key items for the sake of basic knowledge in case you're a novice investor.

Breaking stocks down one level further, you have value, which are stocks that trade at a lower price than what their dividends, sales, and earnings would indicate. For instance, the current dividend yield may be high compared to its historical average. The price to sales or price to earnings ratio may be lower than its historical average as well. Value stocks break down further into large, mid, and small capital as well.

On the other side of the investment table from value are growth stocks. Whereas value stocks are often seen as undervalued, growth stocks can be interpreted more on new ideas, technology, and products. They are more momentum-oriented with a fast-expected growth rate of earnings. They can be a little riskier than value stocks, but the potential could be far greater and well worth the risk. New technology companies are a good example of a growth stock because they possess a lot of potential based on whether or not their product is going to change the world, which happens quite often. Take a look at Amazon, Google, and Facebook, just to name a few.

The smart play for most investors, once again, is diversification, even within stock allocation. By blending some investments in each of the value and growth classifications—both large capitalization and small capitalization—your portfolio becomes smartly balanced.

Bonds

There are also different types of bonds, such as short, intermediate, and long duration; government, corporate, and mortgage-backed; global country, global corporate, and globally blended bonds. Bonds are issued when a company, government, or municipality needs to raise money for a certain purpose. If you invest in bonds, you're basically financing those projects, and are considered a creditor.

As you look at the previously mentioned Ibbotson chart, you might ask, "Why would I ever invest in a bond or a bond fund?" The short answer is, bonds can provide a lower risk component for the portfolio.

Let's say you're retired and drawing 4 percent from your

portfolio for various living expenses. From the goal plan and personal financial policy statement, we would have some percentage of your portfolio in short to intermediate bonds. All monthly draws will come from the bonds. On an annual basis, the portfolio mix would be rebalanced.

This strategy can be most ideal for people who are closer to retirement. If you're younger, you'll likely have nothing in bonds. Instead, you may not want to have everything in equities because you shouldn't need to withdraw for quite a while.

Cash

The last basic building block to discuss is cash, which can be in the form of a money market or certificate of deposit (CD). There's little return but minimal principle volatility with that choice. CDs of less than one year would be considered cash and offer similarly low returns with virtually no principle loss risk. Any CD that is over a year would be considered a bond.

A Typical Breakdown

Consider the value of a carefully devised sample financial goal plan for a fictional couple named Matthew and Mary Client, both age fifty with a desired retirement age of sixty-five.

Current Portfolio Allocation

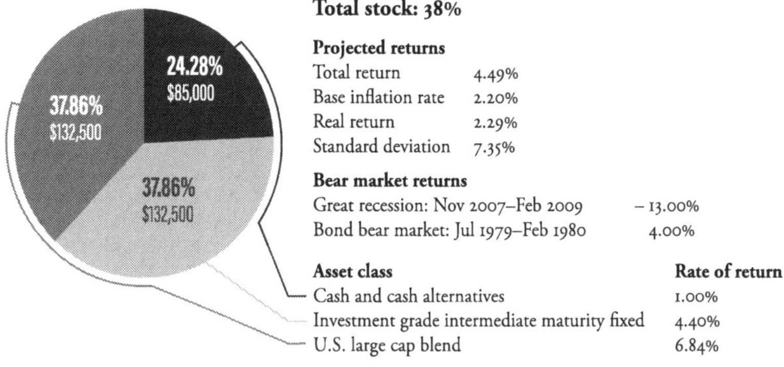

24.28%
$85,000
37.86%
$132,500
37.86%
$132,500
Total stock: 38%
Projected returns
Total return 4.49%
Base inflation rate 2.20%
Real return 2.29%
Standard deviation 7.35%
Bear market returns
Great recession: Nov 2007–Feb 2009 – 13.00%
Bond bear market: Jul 1979–Feb 1980 4.00%
Asset class
Rate of return
Cash and cash alternatives 1.00%
Investment grade intermediate maturity fixed 4.40%
U.S. large cap blend 6.84%

The above is a hypothetical from GPM. The full report can be found in the appendix.

There's a wealth of information in that plan, but if you look at page 8, illustrated here, you'll see the current classification breakdown of investments, including cash, stocks, bonds, and alternatives. You'll also see what their current path is, and what happens to their rate of return when I start to rebalance their portfolio a little more heavily on the stock side of the balance sheet. Consistently, the more money we put into stocks, the greater the return. (See page 10, illustrated here for additional context.)

Portfolio Table

Current	Risk based	Target band	Name	Cash	Bond	Stock	Alternative	Average return Total	Average return Real	Standard deviation
→			Current	24.29%	37.86%	37.86%	0.00%	4.49%	2.29%	7.35%
			Conservative	2.00%	71.00%	27.00%	0.00%	5.10%	2.90%	6.54%
			Conservative Balanced	2.00%	51.00%	47.00%	0.00%	5.60%	3.40%	9.41%
			Balanced	2.00%	31.00%	64.00%	3.00%	6.10%	3.90%	12.31%
	→		Balanced with Growth	2.00%	15.00%	78.00%	5.00%	6.43%	4.23%	14.57%
		→	New Allocation*	0.00%	13.00%	87.00%	0.00%	6.74%	4.54%	16.59%
			Growth	2.00%	0.00%	93.00%	5.00%	6.83%	4.63%	17.21%

**This is a custom portfolio created only for your plan, and the name is for identification purposes only.*

Return vs. Risk Graph

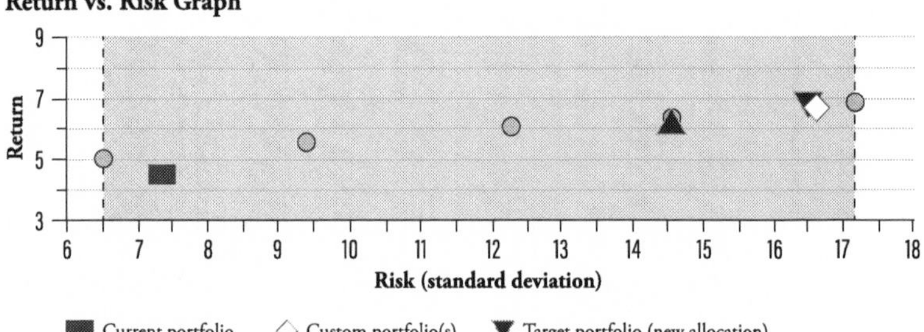

The above is a hypothetical from GPM. The full report can be found in the appendix.

There are many variables to consider in this plan: how the money is invested, what age to retire, and when to take social security. (Take a look at pages 11–24 of the complete financial goal plan in Appendix 1 for details.)

The breakdown of each investment classification we invest in depends largely on client need. Because they're each only fifty years old, they most likely have around fifteen years to go before retirement. Therefore, they may still be best served by investing more heavily in stocks. Our illustration for Matthew and Mary Client is as follows:

Stocks

- Large growth: 17 percent
- Large value: 17 percent
- Small cap growth: 17 percent
- Small cap value: 16 percent
- Developed international: 13 percent
- Total stock investment: 80 percent of portfolio

Bonds

Depending on our view of the bond market, we're not timing bonds but being conservative with them. This isn't the place we're making money. It's a place for stability and withdrawals.

Short to Intermediate Maturity Bonds

- US government/corporate/mortgage: 10 percent
- Note: If in a taxable account, we may also consider tax-free municipal bonds.
- Global (mixture of government/corporate): 3 percent
- Total bond investment: 13 percent of portfolio

Alternative Investments

- Emerging markets: 4 percent
- Global or U.S. real estate, group of commodities: 3 percent

- Total alternative investment: 7 percent of portfolio

The takeaway from all these choices is not to clutter your mind too much by making investing overly complex. Simplicity wins the day again because by going to a financial advisor you trust, you'll get positioned properly to meet your long-term goals. That's where all the hard work you put into choosing the right financial advisor comes in. We live and breathe this stuff. At least, the good ones do. Select a good financial advisor and have them structure a diversified portfolio. The next step is to have some faith in your own ability to create wealth.

Compliance Note: This case study is for illustrative purposes only. Individual cases will vary. Any information is not a complete summary or statement of all available data necessary for making an investment decision and does not constitute a recommendation. Prior to making any investment decision, you should consult with your financial advisor about your individual situation.

The Role of Faith in Wealth Creation

I've known many people in my life who are college-educated, work hard every day, and still struggle mightily to make ends meet. They may be in jobs that don't pay very well, or maybe they've run into some unexpected medical expenses. Anything can happen, but at some point in the struggle, some negative emotions start to creep in—fear, uncertainty, and anxiety, among others. It's human to feel that way, but that's when you need to do your best to defeat those demons of negativity. This is when you need your faith the most.

A passage from the book of Matthew states the following:

> Ask and it will be given to you; seek and you will find; knock and the door will be opened to you. For everyone who asks receives; the one who seeks finds; and to the one who knocks, the door will be opened. (7:6–8)

If you have righteous intent, and you're doing everything you can to put food on the table for your kids, then having faith in God to provide adequately for you may provide the stepping stone you need to get your footing and create wealth. Start with faith in God, find faith within yourself, and then create wealth not only for yourself but for those around you—your children and other family members and friends in need. That will lead to a lasting legacy that will live on for many years past your physical existence on Earth.

My Christian nature has an influence in this belief, but I find that my clients who have faith in God find all kinds of different ways to use their money wisely. Even in retirement, they continue to help those around them. They have a bucket of money that acts like a spring of good intentions. They've lived a life of industriousness and frugality, and now in their retirement years, they're able to do a lot of good with their creation of wealth.

The key thing about faith in Christianity is it's centered around a belief in an afterlife. That idea makes it much easier to have faith and trust in your financial advisor and your own wealth creation because even if it somehow fell apart, it's only temporary. What we have to look forward to after this life is over is far superior to any wealth creation or worldly pleasure we experience in this human existence.

Conversely, I see atheist or agnostic people who are almost always consumed with worry. They worry about their finances, retirement, and more. They lack faith as a principle in their value systems to diminish the negative effects of worry and stress. For my friends who don't share my Christian values, I strongly urge them to write down their value system and let that be their guide to life. Hopefully, it will guide you so you don't have to consume yourselves with worry and fear.

The Six Guiding Investment Principles

Hopefully, once you've created your value system, you'll find some of your values correlate with the six guiding investment principles we use at my firm. The first three, which are trust, patience, and discipline, could all be considered human virtues and are very suitable for your value system.

One of my greatest mentors is Nick Murray, who is an esteemed financial advisor and accomplished author. These six principles, which include the three I just mentioned, plus asset allocation, diversification, and annual rebalancing, are from his teachings. Much like my value list, these principles have never changed. They still hold value twenty years after he initially spoke about them. I mentioned these briefly in the previous chapter, but now I'd like to discuss them in a little more detail to give you a better understanding of their value and what they mean.

Trust

Trust and an unrelenting faith in the future go hand-in-hand. If you have no faith in the future of our planet and humanity, there's no point in investing you hard-earned money at all. There might be a whole litany of problems you see in the world to sour your faith: poverty, domestic violence, war, and others. But in the face of all these problems, you still need to have faith in your ability to succeed.

The atheists of the world always claim if there was a God, none of those things would exist. Everybody would be fed, safe, warm, and happy all the time. However, I think we need those challenges to grow as a species. We all have various hardships in our lives. I've had many of them throughout my many years, but I grew spiritually, emotionally, and psychologically from every one of them.

Financially speaking, trust and faith in the future come down to assuming some level of risk. Don't squirrel your money away in the mattress of your spare bedroom. There's no need to invest it all in gold either because that's almost just as ridiculous. Have some trust in your financial advisor and faith in the world around you. Listen to all of the options presented to you, and in the end, you'll be glad you did.

Patience

We live in an on-demand world, where waiting an extra thirty seconds in the drive-thru lane at McDonalds to get a value meal is a big problem. Just think about businesses like FedEx and Amazon, which quickly rush things through their system to customers. Everything today happens so fast, but not wealth creation. It takes time and patience.

Patience is a virtue, or so they say. It's also something that constantly emanates from people with a peaceful nature. Have you ever met someone who is peaceful but not patient? They're both qualities I see as part of the light side of human nature. Likewise, I associate darkness with chaos and impatience. Lightness, however, I envision as pure peace and patience.

Where patience is required with financial acuity is by understanding that you're going to see your stock investments go down every so often. It's a tough pill to swallow, but it's worth choking it down with a big glass of water, because eventually, market drops are followed by recovery and more growth. Market decreases are temporary. Remember the subprime mortgage mess caused the market to drop significantly. However, the market not only recovered but is now significantly higher. Those investors who were patient enough to wait it out, realizing the market always comes back, have realized a healthy increase of return in their portfolio.

We can't time these issues. Patience, however, is something we can always implement, and eventually, you will be rewarded for it.

Discipline

Earlier, I discussed the concepts of industriousness and frugality. Those are both elements of discipline. As long as you realize that you're in all likelihood not going to win the lottery, it's going to take some hard work and willpower to not live beyond your means.

During my discussion about creating a value list, I mentioned you're going to have to deny yourself something. This is another form of discipline, which is part of frugality. Temptations of modern day life surround us with fancy cars, new homes, shiny electronics, and gadgets galore. We all have different material things that attract us, and discipline isn't about denying yourself every creature comfort available to you, but it is about denying many of them. In short, say yes to moderation and no to excess.

It's also important not to sell yourself short when evaluating your own discipline. Meeting with a financial planner is generally not the most fun thing in the world to do. So just by taking the time out of your busy day to talk with an advisor about your financial future, you're exhibiting a very important form of discipline.

If something is of particular importance to you, work hard, save for it, and go get it. Just make sure it doesn't affect your ability to plan smartly for your future. That's where discipline is involved.

Asset Allocation

The term "asset allocation" sounds so unnecessarily complex. In laymen's terms, it's all the different places where your money is invested.

According to *Investor Words Glossary*, "asset allocation" is simply defined as the process of dividing investments among different types of assets, such as stocks, bonds, real estate, commodities, and cash to optimize the risk/reward tradeoff based on your specific situation and goals.

The first thing a financial advisor needs to know about a client is if they're an investor or a saver. An investor may take a few more risks, whereas a saver just wants to keep growing their portfolio at a steady rate with little to no risk at all.

All participants should think like an investor, not a saver. A saver is all about cash, money markets, CDs, and bonds. I'm speaking to the wealth-builder here, not so much the retired person.

A key point to remember on the return side of things is where you have your money over any length of time is the return you will get. Refer back to the Ibbotson chart for a good depiction. In other words, for a long-term investment, look at the returns, understand the risks, and set a strategy to reach the specific goals. That's the essence of creating a plan to reach your goals.

Blending the right mix of stocks, bonds, real estate, commodities, and cash is how effective asset allocation works. It's the key to investment success. Financial advisors should have a great amount of knowledge here. Again, find a competent advisor for the best results in your portfolio.

Diversification

If your assets aren't allocated properly—if they're too concentrated in one or two investments—you can find yourself in a higher risk position than you should be. For example, I had a client who had all his wealth in one company. He didn't want to sell any of his position because he would have had to pay the 15 percent capital gains tax. My strong advice was for him to consider some diversification strategies to diversify this holding. In simple terms, I implored him to reallocate into a more diversified portfolio. Despite my best efforts, he ignored my advice and stuck to his unbalanced portfolio. Unfortunately for my client, his unwillingness to pay the taxes caused him to lose a bundle of money when the stock lost 30 percent in one day.

As it turns out, if he would have rebalanced the way I recommended and paid the taxes accordingly, he would have been way ahead of where he was after the disastrous stock drop.

Getting rich quick is not what prudent financial advisors are about—whether you're an investor, a saver, or somewhere in-between. Either way, we're going to come up with a plan based on historical data over twenty, thirty, or forty-year periods that will smartly diversify your portfolio to reach your stated objectives and goals.

REBALANCING

Clients may confuse the concept of rebalancing with timing. We don't time the markets at all, but we do rebalance your portfolio annually based on a written personal financial policy statement.

Timing involves gazing into a crystal ball and trying to predict exactly what day and time each stock or fund is going to rise and fall, which is impossible to do with any sustained success. The normal method of our rebalancing involves buying things out of cycle. A good example of this is in the investment years 2015 and 2016.

At the end of 2015, growth performed a lot better than value stocks. Therefore, we sold the growth and rebalanced into value. In other words, we sold the growth position, which had large returns, and purchased the value position, which had poor returns. At the end of next year, the reverse happened, where value was performing better than growth. So our clients reaped the rewards of the previous rebalancing, and then we rebalanced back out of value and into growth again.

Rebalancing is a very basic concept of investing. The

process is determined from the existing personal financial policy statement, which was built from our Monte Carlo planning process, where we run all the numbers to determine how you will reach your goals. No market timing is involved in this process, and that is a very key point to remember.

Reader Notes

Write down notes to your children (or other loved ones) about the importance of creating wealth.

Chapter Five

Managing and Protecting Wealth

That man is richest whose pleasures are cheapest.

—HENRY DAVID THOREAU

As I mentioned previously, financial advisors are not soothsayers. When you're young, our goal is to establish a life plan for you so you can create wealth. When you get older—fifty-five years old or thereabouts—your goals change, and we establish a plan to manage and protect your wealth. Many times, this idea of managing boils down to the behavioral aspect of our job.

A Tale of Two Investment Strategies

Is there such a thing as a perfect investment? Not really, but some definitely seem more perfect than others. Let's examine two strategies of investing $100,000. One is with a twenty-year bond, and the other is a growing dividend stock portfolio.

The Twenty-Year Bond

Let's say you decide to buy a twenty-year bond for $100,000, and it pays a generous yield of 5 percent. Elementary math says you'll earn $5,000 per year you can use for living expenses. After the twenty years is up, you get your $100,000 back, but when inflation is factored in (for our illustration, we'll use 2.2 percent), it's actually worth $64,711.59. An added detractor to this strategy is, at this point, you also need to consider renewal, which may involve either higher or lower interest rates.

Two Investments Compared: First Investment

Bond
Buy a 20-year bond paying 5% interest per year. Bond purchased at par and redeemed fully at par at maturity in 20 years.

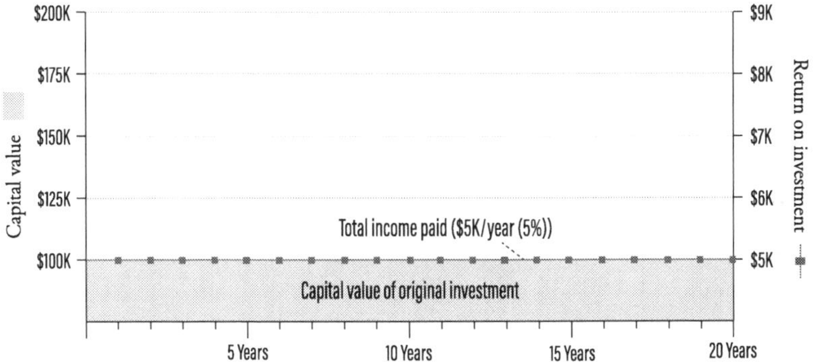

- Start: Purchase $100,000 20-year bond.
- Income paid and spent per year: $5,000.
- Therefore, $5,000 was paid each year until bond matured.

This is a hypothetical illustration and is not intended to reflect the actual performance of any particular security. Future performance cannot be guaranteed, and investment yields will fluctuate with market conditions.

The Growing Dividend Stock Portfolio

Another choice for your $100,000 investment would be a growing dividend stock portfolio. Let's say you invested your money in twenty-five high-quality companies who have paid and grown their dividends every year for several years. Furthermore, we'll estimate the total dividend payout is around 3 percent for this portfolio. That means the dividend paid to you in year one will be $3,000. However, the nature of a growing dividend stock portfolio is growth. Our elementary math tells us that's $2,000 less per year for living expenses than with the bond in year one.

Two Investments Compared: Second Investment

Growing dividend stock portfolio (GDSP)

Invest in 25 companies paying/growing dividends at a current dividend percentage of 3%.

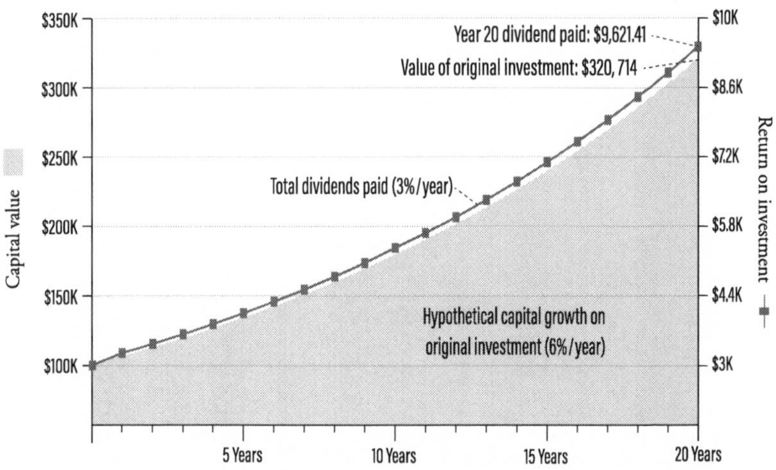

This investment does not have a stated maturity date. The income therefore can continue and has grown to 9.6% of the original investment.

This is a hypothetical illustration and is not intended to reflect the actual performance of any particular security. Future performance cannot be guaranteed, and investment yields will fluctuate with market conditions.

Compliance Note: This is a hypothetical situation and is not intended to reflect the actual performance of any particular security. Future performance cannot be guaranteed, and investment yields will fluctuate with market conditions. Actual investor results will vary.

If the average rate of dividends paid increases by 6 percent per year for all twenty years, then in year twenty, the amount of dividends paid is $9,621.41. Let's also say the capital appreciation of the stocks is 6 percent per year. Therefore, 3 percent is paid out for living expenses, and the growth of capital remains in the account. This would indicate the pot of money would have grown to $320,714.

Compliance Note: Dividends are not guaranteed and must be authorized by the company's board of directors.

Does the growing dividend stock portfolio sound too good to be true?

Maybe you don't believe my numbers?

You might even doubt the realism of the rates I used in my calculations?

Well, the good news is that it's all true, and my numbers are actually far more conservative than what recent performance would indicate as your likely results. Consider for a reference point, if we use the return of the Dividend Aristocrats actual performance from February 2, 1989, through December 31, 2015, the rate was 13.4 percent, which of course would increase the value substantially more. Notice how conservative my estimate is, and it still blows away the bond strategy!

Which strategy would you rather own? Choice A is the bond, where you get your money back and $5,000 per year over twenty years. Choice B is the growing dividend stock portfolio, where you get a steadily increasing amount of income over twenty years, in which the amount is almost double of Choice A by the end of the term. Plus, you get a capital base that has grown to almost triple. If you made a decision for one of these portfolios twenty years ago, which portfolio would you like to have chosen?

Compliance Note: This assumes a stock driven portfolio meets the investment objectives and risk tolerance over that for a particular investor.

What to Do with Your 401(k) Post-Retirement

Now that you have an understanding of one investment strategy and why stocks are normally a better choice than bonds, I'd like to discuss another investment strategy that involves your 401(k) plan.

What can you do with your 401(k) balance? A good financial advisor will be able to look through the cost structure of the specific plan, factor in your life goals and objectives, and help you to make a good decision.

If you haven't already secured a financial advisor, make sure you find one several years before retirement and have this discussion with them. It is important to map out how to reach your goals and objectives for retirement to determine what the right path is for your 401(k) plan.

The thing to remain aware of in this scenario is most financial advisors can't keep your business if they tell you to keep your money in a 401(k) plan. They can't be compensated with fees for advice regarding it. So you can leave the money in your plan, but you'll still have to deal with the management of the portfolio.

If you choose to take your money out of the 401(k) plan, you can roll it over to a tax-deferred IRA. From your plan, the proceeds can be invested to reach your goals. You should, however, consider all your available options and the applicable fees and features of each before moving your retirement assets. Remember, you have more than a few options to consider, which we discussed in detail in Chapter 1.

Compliance Note: In addition to rolling over your 401(k) to an IRA, there are other options. For additional information and what is suitable for your particular situation, please consult a qualified financial advisor. Here is a brief look at all your options:

- Leave money in your former employer's plan, if permitted.
    - Pros: If you like the investments in the plan, you get to stay in them and you may not incur a fee for leaving it in the plan. This choice does not constitute a taxable event.

- If you weren't retiring, but just leaving the company, you could roll over the assets to your new employer's plan, if one is available and it is permitted.
    - Pros: You can keep it all together and have a larger sum of money working for you. This also does not constitute a taxable event.
    - Con: Not all employer plans accept rollovers.
- Rollover to an IRA.
    - Pros: You likely have more investment options. It allows for consolidation of accounts and locations. This also does not constitute a taxable event.
    - Cons: There is usually a fee involved. There could also be potential fees for termination.
- Cash out the account.
- Cons: Cashing out is a taxable event and there is a potential for loss of investments. This is a costly option for individuals under fifty-nine-and-one-half years of age because it involves a 10 percent penalty in addition to being subject to applicable income taxes.

If you elect to roll the money out of your 401(k) plan and into an investment option under the management of an advisory firm, then the financial advisor can go over your strategy throughout retirement. They will map out a plan for you into your nineties. With advances in healthcare, they may need to move these numbers higher. However, they plan to meet standards above the standard mortality tables. Nonetheless, I know plenty of people within my own inner circle who are over ninety years old, so running numbers to that age makes plenty of sense. For example, my mother is a young ninety-three years old, and her mother lived to 106!

A Case Study in Retirement Planning

Let's plan out the hypothetical situation of a couple, age sixty-six, planning for retirement with around $1 million in after-tax savings to work with. It's likely they have some money in a 401(k) plan and social security benefits as well, and they'll also have a spending budget to consider. All those items will be discussed in our planning process. What we're going to discuss now, however, is how we'll invest that $1 million in after-tax savings.

The precise mix of their exact investments will vary somewhat depending on several factors, including the full planning process, their Monte Carlo analysis, and their personal financial policy statement (PFPS). Most likely, we'll recommend a mix of investments like the following.

After-Tax (Taxable) Investments

- A growing dividend stock portfolio of twenty-five high-quality companies with a track record of paying dividends every year and the potential for capital appreciation. This will likely include large capitalization growth stocks and large capitalization value stocks.

- Managed municipal bonds (general obligation and revenue) or high-quality managed taxable bonds (short and intermediate), as well as taxable bonds (US government, mortgage-backed, corporate, international, and global).
- Exchange-traded funds (ETFs), such as small capitalization and international companies. These investment choices will include developed international markets like Europe and Japan, and emerging markets from the BRIC countries (Brazil, Russia, India, and China, plus others). ETFs could be either actively or passively managed and may include investments in real estate and commodities as well.

IRA (Tax-Deferred) Investments

Since IRAs are tax-deferred and taxes are not an issue for portfolio management, we would most likely create a diversified portfolio of institutional mutual funds, diversified by asset class (stocks, bonds, and cash) and style (large capitalization growth, large capitalization value, small capitalization growth, small capitalization value, developed international, emerging markets, global/U.S. real estate, and a basket of commodities).

As far as their 401(k) or IRA money is concerned in this

example, they can let their IRA money grow without any withdrawals until they're seventy and one-half years old. That's when the required minimum distribution (RMD) rules come into play. At that point, they can elect to spend the distribution or slide these funds over into their taxable portfolio to build even more income for their existing and future lifestyle.

What about Roth?

Another item this couple might consider is moving money from their IRA to a Roth IRA, which may be beneficial to maximize a current lower tax bracket.

For a young person, especially if they're in a lower tax bracket, contributing to a Roth 401(k) or Roth IRA is very appealing. For a retired person, they may want to consider moving money from their IRA to a Roth IRA again, especially if they're in a lower tax bracket. Remember, Roth 401(k) or Roth IRAs distributions come out income-tax free. This can be a wonderful type of account.

Protecting Wealth

Protecting wealth comes down to three elements: performance, risk, and taxes.

- **Performance:** You need to ensure your investments

are performing adequately enough to continue providing income during retirement. Think of growing income at or above the rate of inflation.

- **Risk:** At the same time, you need to minimize risk to ensure your retirement doesn't disappear.
- **Taxes:** You should try to organize your financial assets to minimize tax implications. Being foolish with your portfolio could result in paying too much in taxes, which could quickly erode your portfolio and negatively affect your comfort level during retirement.

Fortunately, financial advisors have access to several great financial research providers. They provide information that enables firms like mine to investigate which funds are performing up to par and which ones aren't. For instance, I can look at every large-capitalization growth manager in the known universe to find out which ones have been in the top 30 percent in any timeframe I deem worthwhile. I can break it down into one, three, five, ten, and fifteen years if I want to. At that point, I should be able to choose which active or passive managers are best suited for my clients.

A good financial advisor understands how capital markets work. They sort through all the available financial research and provide their clients with sound investment management. The financial advisor reviews all data, such things as standard deviation, beta, sharp ratios, alpha, etc.

The financial advisor also looks at the investment management teams and makes sure the people responsible for the portfolio performance are still working for the fund you are considering.

We Can't Save You from Yourself

Performance and risk are both tied tightly to the idea of trust in your financial advisor because it's easy to lose that trust if you see either a lack of performance or unacceptably high risk in your portfolio.

As retirement approaches within ten to fifteen years, it becomes increasingly important to have trust at the heart of your relationship with your financial advisor. If that's not there, you could find yourself in a situation like a client of mine who didn't trust us enough to follow our advice when turmoil struck, which it inevitably does every five to seven years. Keep in mind with all the scenarios in this book, the names and other variables have been altered for privacy concerns.

This client of mine was fifty-eight years old back in 2016 when Brexit happened. To put it mildly, it scared the life out of him. He had over $1 million invested smartly in one of our portfolios we set up for him.

When Brexit formally happened, he called in a panic wanting to know if we were watching the news. He thought it was going to be a major thing and wanted out. We told him to relax and did our best to calm him down by providing him with all sorts of historical data.

He called at least three times before, finally, he couldn't take it anymore, and he moved 100 percent of his beautifully diversified, long-term, goal-oriented portfolio into cash. We told him once he did that, we weren't going to tell him when to move it back (other than move it back immediately) because nobody can truly predict with any real accuracy when the best time is to do that.

He realized a few weeks later—along with everybody else—that Brexit wasn't going to cause mass hysteria and a global economic meltdown. It was just another blip on the radar screen of financial history. So we put him back into something else (again, not what we recommended though), and the results are as follows:

- The rate of return on his investments at the end of 2016 was 1.02 percent.
- If he stayed in our portfolio, which was 80 percent stocks and 20 percent bonds, he would have received an 11.71 percent return. That equates to a net loss of 10.69 percent.
- When applied to the value of his investments, the total dollar value of the net loss for him by making that one

critical error against the best advice from his advisor was over $115,000.

The bottom line is, refer to the six principles: trust, patience, discipline, asset allocation, diversification, and annual rebalancing. Think of a way to incorporate these principles and be confident they will guide you correctly.

This person is still a very valued client and he understands his mistake today, but that understanding isn't going to recoup his loss. I would never approach any valued clients with an attitude of "I told you so." But I do need to take the opportunity to explain to people when and where they went wrong so it doesn't happen again. My worst fear is that a client makes such an awful and costly mistake like this one more than once.

It's also worth noting that this client didn't do much worse than the average investor has over the past twenty years. Most people make around 2.3 percent annual return on their investments, according to this corresponding Dalbar study.

Twenty-Year Annualized Returns by Asset Class (1997–2016)

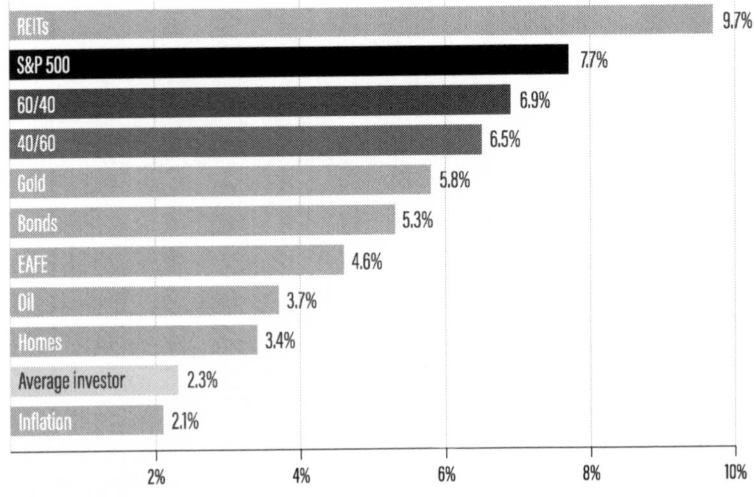

Source: J.P. Morgan Asset Management; Dalbar Inc.
Indexes used are as follows: REITS: NAREIT Equity REIT index; 60/40: a balanced portfolio with 60% invested in S&P 500 Index and 40% invested in high quality U.S. fixed income, represented by the Barclays U.S. Aggregate Index; Gold: USD/troy oz.; Bonds: Barclays U.S. Aggregate Index; EAFE: MSCI EAFE; Oil: WTI Index; Homes: median sale price of existing single-family homes; Inflation: CPI. The portfolio is rebalanced annually. Average asset allocation investor return is based on an analysis by Dalbar Inc., which utilizes the net of aggregate mutual fund sales, redemptions and exchanges each month as a measure of investor behavior. Returns are annualized (and total return where applicable) and represent the 20-year period ending December 31, 2016, to match Dalbar's most recent analysis.
Guide to the Markets – U.S. Data are as of December 31, 2017.

Compliance Note: This case study is for illustrative purposes only. Individual cases will vary. Any information is not a complete summary or statement of all available data necessary for making an investment decision and does not constitute a recommendation. Prior to making any investment decision, you should consult with your financial advisor about your individual situation.

The typical 60/40 diversified portfolio, however, is currently making around 6.9 percent. This client had the unfortunate occurrence of doing worse than the average investor in a year where most diversified portfolios did even better than average. But if you're incorrectly diversified, you may have not obtained the proper return, and that's why choosing a financial advisor you trust is so valuable.

WHAT ARE BONDS GOOD FOR?

How do investors who fear the market with such extreme intensity become more confident with their portfolio? They can make more stable choices. I don't usually recommend bonds as anything more than a stabilizer in a portfolio, but if you are truly fearful of such events, a higher percentage of bonds may be a good fit for your individual investment strategy.

High-quality bonds can provide preservation against stock market volatility. Therefore, you don't want your bonds to be correlated to stocks in any regard. The only thing worse than watching your stock portfolio plummet due to a financial crisis is if you have 50 percent of your money in bonds, thinking they're less volatile, only to find out they performed like stocks during the market drop. The result of such a situation is that your entire portfolio drops, which is a terrible situation to live through. Therefore, keep your bonds on their own side of the equation, which is away from the stocks. Think of it like separating the two kids in school who can't be together without getting into trouble.

The other thing to remember about investing in bonds is their association with interest rates. For instance, if Wall Street is expecting a faster growing economy and rising interest rates, that usually means we need to be careful about long-term bonds. Remember, interest rates and bonds have an inverse relationship. If interest rates go up, bond prices will go down. Also, note that longer maturity bonds will decrease in value more than short maturity bonds when interest rates go up.

When managed appropriately, bonds are ideally suited for stability by protecting short-term principle loss. We still recommend not falling in love with them and putting the majority of your portfolio in stocks, but bonds serve a purpose in a well-balanced portfolio, which is minimizing principle loss and risk, while providing a stable resource of money.

If you are retired or getting close to it, you may have a 30 percent allocation in bonds, which you'll use to withdraw from for living expenses. The reason for a 30 percent allocation is if you have a $1 million portfolio, that means $300,000 is in bonds, which could give you years of cash withdrawal resources. At a 4 percent withdrawal rate, you'll have seven-and-a-half years of stable cash available before any rebalancing is done.

Stock Diversification Helps to Lower Your Volatility

Minimizing risk isn't all about buying bonds of different classifications. It can also be accomplished with a smart balance of large and small-capitalization stocks. We like the large-capitalization-small-capitalization mix because there is some correlated difference between the two groups. Again, we urge portfolio diversification.

Extending that diversification into foreign markets is also a good option. You should have some money in developed international markets, generally focused in Europe and Japan. You should also invest some percentage of your portfolio in emerging markets, such as the BRIC countries, which is Brazil, Russia, India, and China. It's beneficial to have more diversification in other emerging economies that may be on the verge of sprouting.

What about Taxes?

Individual stocks can be much more beneficial than owning mutual funds in a taxable portfolio from a tax standpoint. Pick twenty, twenty-five, or thirty individual companies to invest in and collect the dividends. If you never sell those stocks, you'll never have to pay capital gains. But it's hard to own one company for your lifetime, so paying capital gains tax is expected. Both dividends and capital gains—as of this writing—are currently taxed at 15 percent if you're a married couple with income under $450,000. If your income is over $450,000, capital gains and dividends are taxed at 20 percent.

Compliance Note: Changes in tax laws may occur at any time and could have a substantial impact on each person's situation. You should discuss tax or legal matters with the appropriate professional.

In a perfect world, you would like to pick twenty-five companies in a growing dividend stock portfolio and hold them for your lifetime. However, you still need to buy and sell different positions from time to time, because some companies will either make poor management decisions or the transformative world may cause some disruption in their industry. (Consider future technological and process changes, e.g., Amazon versus brick-and-mortar stores, etc.)

Both dividends and capital gains are tax advantaged. Also, if you did hold a position for your entire life, it would include a stepped-up cost basis with no capital gains for your heirs. You could also execute something called "wash sales" in an individual stock portfolio.

An example of a wash sale would be if you have $10,000 year-to-date capital gains in your portfolio but one position with a $6,000 loss, you could sell the position and wipe out $6,000 from the overall gain. Thirty-one days later, you could buy the position back. That works well if the position sold stays at the same value or decreases in value during the next thirty-one days before you buy it back.

Insurance: The First Line of Defense

Many American households today consist of two working parents, a couple of kids, and a mortgage payment. What's needed at this early stage of your financial life is protection, and in most cases, insurance needs to be part of the equation. In other words, you may need a life insurance policy to serve as the first line of defense in case something tragic happens to you, leaving your spouse to raise the kids and pay all the bills alone. Ideally, you want to have a policy that at least pays off the mortgage and provides a roof over your loved ones' heads when you're gone.

Insurance, however, is not meant to serve as retirement income. Some clients come to me with fourteen different insurance policies and think they're going to retire on it, but that's not going to happen. Get a smart policy that covers you for your most critical time of life, which is when you have young children to care for and a mortgage to pay. You can accomplish this with a term policy. Others prefer the comfort and total coverage of a permanent life insurance policy. Either one is fine, but make sure you're covered for your own individual needs.

A young family with young kids to care for is usually best served with an effective term policy. In about 99 percent of the cases, I've encountered a good term policy provided a cost-effective way for a young couple to protect their family. However, occasionally there is a need for more coverage. Permanent insurance comes into play when a larger estate is at stake. It's usually best served for wealthy clientele with heirs and charities to consider, and it can also be a good way to accomplish tax mitigation.

Long-Term Care Insurance

As you get older, you have to make a decision about long-term care insurance. This is one of the larger financial risks to consider. Long-term care insurance should be discussed in-depth with all family members to provide true peace of mind for everyone involved.

One option is to forego any type of policy for long-term care, which requires you to assume responsibility for any nursing home care later in life. That may be the best option to use. Once your money is gone, you will be a ward of the state with tax payers footing your long-term care bill. A lot of people accept this option because they simply can't afford the insurance anyway. In essence, the decision is made for them.

Some people may choose to hide their wealth and burden the taxpayers with their long-term care, despite their healthy financial situation. That's not a very Christian thing to do, and you would need a financial advisor who supports such a decision. Most ethical advisors, however, will not agree to such a strategy.

Three other choices for long-term care exist as well:

1. You could purchase long-term care insurance.
2. You could also choose to convert your existing permanent life insurance policy into a new policy, which can be used for long-term care.
3. Or you could purchase a new life insurance policy that offers the death benefit to be paid out for long-term care benefits. Many people like this option because the premiums paid will benefit someone, either their own long-term care needs or a death benefit paid to their heirs.

Remember, however, you do need to pass the insurance company's physical to qualify for either of these options.

Umbrella Coverage

An umbrella policy is designed to protect your wealth against major claims and lawsuits. It goes beyond the coverage provided by your homeowners, auto, and boat policies. For example, let's say you're a seventy-nine-year-old client with $5 million in total assets and a $500,000 liability auto insurance policy. What happens if you get into a car accident with a mom who has three kids in the back seat, and one of them tragically dies? Most likely, your insurance company will write a check for the full $500,00 almost immediately. Additionally, the heartbroken parents are also likely to hire an attorney who is going to sue you for every penny of your $5 million in assets, and they're probably going to get it. For a very reasonable fee, however, an umbrella policy will cover you in such an unfortunate circumstance. I highly recommend this coverage option.

Extending Wealth to Future Generations

After you've sufficiently created and protected your wealth, the true beauty is in being able to extend it to future generations. When you think about extending wealth, you might think about your kids and grandkids. Other people might think their kids make more money than they ever made and they don't need to leave them anything. There's no right or wrong way to do it. Whatever feels right to you is the way God meant for you to extend your wealth.

You have options if you decide to set some things up for future generations. There are 529 college funding programs that can be enormously beneficial to giving future generations a leg up in the world by allowing them to get their college education without being indebted to student loans for the rest of their lives. Beyond that, you can set up trust funds and leave valuable items in your will.

It's important to obtain and meet with a competent estate planning attorney to design the proper estate plan that meets your forward generation financial planning goals. If you created wealth, doesn't it make sense to move your wealth ahead to future generations to do more good things? Start with a serious conversation with your trusted financial advisor. They can move this important issue in the right direction for you.

Extending wealth is a wonderful notion, but it starts with creation and protection. If you're not smart with your decisions during those phases of your life, then your legacy may be affected later on, and perhaps you won't have extending wealth as an option. I like to think all of us have the ability to make it happen, and as long as we make smart choices during our most productive years, anything is possible.

Reader Notes

Write down notes to your children (or other loved ones) about the importance of protecting wealth.

Chapter Six

Building a Legacy

Someone is sitting in the shade today because long ago someone planted a tree.

—WARREN BUFFETT

What do you think of when you think about your legacy?

Do you think about money, your heirs, or charities near and dear to your heart?

Or do you think about your good intentions, positive actions, and words of wisdom extending through future generations long after you're gone?

I think of my legacy as all those things. There's a financial side to it, but the larger aspect of my legacy is the one that extends far beyond mere finances. It's my spiritual legacy, and it will live on forever in the hearts and minds of future generations whom my thoughts, actions, and wisdom have impacted.

Your Spiritual Legacy

When I open my eyes for the first time every morning and get ready to embrace another day full of the wonders God has provided, I start by reciting the following words:

> I love my church, all churches, and all people. I love myself too, which is very important. After all, without love of thyself, how else is it possible to love others?
>
> I love God, Jesus, the Holy Spirit, and the Virgin Mary, who is one of the reasons I was given life. By her grace, love, and sacrifices, I was not aborted, and I was given the chance for a long and loving life through wonderfully caring and nurturing parents. I also love all the saints who were martyred for their beliefs. I don't worship them, I worship God, but I recognize them, and hope to have even a grain of the faith they had in their lifetimes.
>
> Like St. Jude, who professed hope and belief in miracles, and St. Francis of Assisi, who said to go out and evangelize, but only use words when necessary, I hope to positively impact the lives of others with my undying faith and altruistic actions.

As we lead up to the financial aspect of your legacy, I'd like you to envision a fork in the road. Let's call it Legacy Road. If you choose the path to the left, you'll create just enough wealth to spend every last dollar until you pass away. You'll leave nothing behind, and therefore, no more financial wealth exists from your days on Earth.

The path to the right, however, is different. That is one where you decide to preserve as much of your estate as possible. Along that path, your wealth grows to provide you income, as well as capital to leave to heirs and worthy charities for many years and perhaps many generations after you're gone.

Which Road Is the Road to Greed?

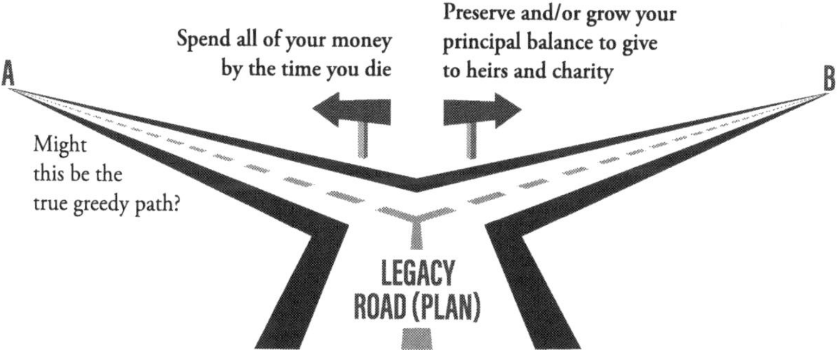

One of the paths on Legacy Road I described is the path of greed. The other path is the path of non-greed. Which one do you think is which?

Most people would likely answer that the path of greed is

the one where you're growing as much wealth as possible, trying to accumulate more and more for every step you take on Earth. Those same people would likely draw the conclusion that the path of non-greed is the one where you're creating just enough wealth to spend for your own existence and pass away with nothing left.

I, however, would argue just the opposite of most people's interpretation of this fork in Legacy Road. In my mind, the path where you create just enough wealth for yourself and leaving nothing to anyone else is the greedy one. By contrast, the one where you work hard to tithe and grow as much wealth as possible, not for your own best interest, but for the well-being of future generations and people in need around the world is the path of non-greed. That's the direction I want to go in, and I sincerely hope you do too.

Your Financial Legacy (Consider a Charitable Trust or a Donor Advised Fund)

In a wonderful way, your financial legacy can be tied to your spiritual legacy. By creating a donor advised fund (DAF), your generosity and dedication to contributing to the greater good of the human spirit can last for many generations. A DAF is a philanthropic endeavor you can establish that allows donors to make contributions at any time, while receiving an immediate tax benefit for yourself.

Subsequently, grants from the fund can be given to various charitable organizations by the trustees of the fund.

As the trustee of the DAF, you decide where the money goes, and it can be as much or as little as you like, as opposed to the charitable trust, where you have to donate 5 percent or more every year. You can also name who the successors of the DAF will be after you've passed. In other words, you can declare your children will be the ones who decide what money goes to which charity. When they're gone, they can name their children, and so on. In that way, your philanthropic spirit can live virtually forever!

The establishment of a charitable family trust or DAF can be very beneficial for mitigating taxes for two reasons:

1. **Low-cost stocks:** You can contribute the shares of your low-cost stocks to your charitable trust or DAF and forego paying the capital gains tax, which could be 15 or 20 percent.
2. **Full value:** In most cases, the full value of the contribution can be a full deduction from your income. (It must satisfy the 30/50 percent rule.) If you are unable to deduct the full amount in the current tax year because of this rule, you can carry the remaining amount forward to deduct in a future year.

Compliance Note: Contributions to a Donor Advised Fund are irrevocable.

DEFINITION OF THE 30/50 PERCENT RULE

You may deduct charitable contributions of money or property made to qualified organizations if you itemize your deductions. Generally, you may deduct up to 50 percent of your adjusted gross income, but 20 percent and 30 percent limitations apply in some cases. For further clarification on this, refer to IRS Code 170.

The financial aspect of your legacy is probably the easiest part to plan. It really all depends on what needs to be planned. What type of estate are you leaving? For complex estate planning, I advise you find a competent estate attorney to work in conjunction with your financial advisor. The estate attorney should understand all the nuances, tax laws, and potential benefits for the estate to be passed on to your heirs or charity. Also, a competent CPA should be on your legacy planning team.

Consider the following questions when planning for both the financial and spiritual aspects of your legacy, and maybe make some notes accordingly in the "Reader Notes" section that follows:

- How do you want to be remembered?
- Are you living in a way God intended, which is to be the best you can possibly be?

- Will you be able to leave this world in a better place by creating enough financial wealth for your family and future generations?
- Did you create your wealth honestly and with great integrity?

Many times, when I think about legacy, I'm reminded of the movie *Saving Private Ryan*. It's an epic war movie with a very valuable life lesson. The movie closes with Private Ryan at the graveside of his dear friend and hero, Captain Miller. After gazing at the site for several moments, he utters some of the most heart-wrenching and emotionally charged words in the history of moviemaking, tearfully saying to his wife, "Tell me I'm a good man."

Private Ryan is obviously aware of the sacrifices Captain Miller and his men made for him. In the end, what he needs is validation that his actions, his impact in the world, and perhaps his legacy justified their sacrifice.

I urge all of us to think in a similar fashion. Live your life in a purposeful way, recognize and appreciate the sacrifices others have made before you, and try to leave the world a better place through your own thoughts and actions. Make that your legacy, and you will live forever as royalty in the minds of everyone your kind and generous spirit embraced.

Reader Notes

Write down notes to your children (or other loved ones) about the importance of legacy planning.

Conclusion

Four Blessings, Over a Lifetime

He was given life from a tough beginning and was blessed many times over. With our God, nothing is impossible.

—MARK A. AHO

My value system is what helps me to be true to myself. At its core are three rocks of my existence: God, my wife, and my children. Their blessed influence serves as my continued inspiration behind the twelve values I mentioned earlier in the book. Those values have never changed, and every time I see myself getting perhaps a little off the rails, I refer back to those values, and the answer to whatever was troubling me suddenly becomes crystal clear.

Every day is a new opportunity to do something wonderful. Take some time to write out a value system, and you'll discover new ways to create some magic every day, either for yourself, your children, or others around you. Your value system doesn't need to be twelve items long. It might be only five or ten. Maybe it will be more like twenty or twenty-five. The number of values isn't important, but it's important to stay true to them because they will guide you to where you want to be.

Key Takeaways

As I begin to wrap up my exploration of living a life of faith and basic financial wisdom, you should understand the gist of this book is not to merely provide raw financial data and execute financial transactions based on those numbers. There are plenty of books available with all that information.

My purpose for writing this book is more about basic life lessons, extending advice to your children so they can live fruitfully and serve God responsibly, and hopefully, some sound financial planning got through as well. Please consider the following key takeaways from each chapter as a summary of what you just read and consider passing the information on to future generations of your family.

Preface

- If you haven't constructed your own personal value

system through honesty and good intentions, how are you going to be able to stay on track for just about any goal you set for yourself? If you reach a particular goal, will it even be meaningful?

- Sit down in a quiet space and put your value system on paper. If done correctly, it will virtually never change. When you're done writing it all down, laminate it and carry it with you to keep your train on the right set of tracks.
- Procrastination is not your friend. Don't put off acting upon the lessons you learned from this book. Yes, it may take a lot of effort, but the results will be well worth it. After all, anything worth doing is going to be at least a little challenging.

Introduction: Four Blessings

- Do you know your life is a gift? Have you truly thought about life in such a way?
- What about your family, like your mom, dad, sisters, brothers, aunts, and uncles? What about your closest friends? Think about how important these people are in your life. Have you told them lately—or ever—that you love them? If not, what are you waiting for? Get going.
- A thankful heart is a happy heart. If you're sad, angry, discouraged, or even depressed, think of something you're thankful for. Do it with me now and anytime

you're feeling that way, and those negative thoughts and emotions will exit your consciousness. Hmm...I'm feeling better already!

- Positive energy attracts more positive energy. Negative energy attracts more negative energy. The good news is that we get to choose the type of energy we want. Which would be your choice?
- Where is your faith? How are you and God getting along? Are you willing to reach out to someone or something greater than you? Faith is the key to all miracles. Do you feel like you need a miracle? Are you going to just let life go by, or are you going to immerse yourself in the richness of our creator's grace?
- Do you feel like a failure? Are you just getting by? Or are you very comfortable and don't want to disturb anything at this time? If you're successful, do you know why? Or are you transformative, blazing new trails and having the time of your life by being so successful you can affect the lives of others in an abundantly positive way?

Chapter One: The Story Changes, but Truths Remain

- Humility builds future success if you can look at a humiliating incident as a learning experience. Think about embarrassing failures in your life. You probably learned a lot from them. People willing to try new things and to take some risks are learning and growing. Those who are afraid of taking any risk don't have the opportunity to grow as much or learn as quickly. So take a deep breath, think carefully about the endeavor, and take that first step. You can do it!

- Do you have the discipline to deny yourself something you really want? Can you live on less money than what you earn? I believe those who take risks, work hard, and never give up on their goals are doing everything they can to see their dreams come true. They may not acquire every creature comfort they desire along the way, but in the end, they will have achieved far more. Just remember, there are no free lunches.
- Tend to your own garden. Don't worry about the gardens of others, which may include greater wealth, more possessions, and the appearance of a grandiose lifestyle. If you take good care of what is in front of you, it will grow as long as you nurture it with strong faith and believe in your own abilities to succeed.
- Do not overspend on your house for the amount of income you have. A house is not necessarily an investment. It's a place for you and your family to live and call home. You need to make other investments to create wealth, provide for your retirement, and potentially make charitable donations.
- It is never too early to start planning for the future. Start thinking now about such life events as your kids' college educations, your retirement, and your legacy.

Chapter Two: Making Wealth Purposeful

- It is so important to know the why before the how. At this moment of your life, if you're trying to do something and you don't know why or have a passionate reason behind your actions, it's likely the result won't make a lot of sense or make much of a positive impact.
- If you have not sat down and listed your specific future goals, you should start now. You may have an aha moment. My advice is to find a good financial advisor to walk you through this.
- Remember the five bags of gold story and don't be afraid. Don't be the servant who buried his money. If you're not sure how to make your garden grow like the other servants, then seek a financial advisor to help you.

Chapter Three: Choosing the Right Advisor

- Interview at least three financial advisors to ensure the one you select is someone you believe in and trust.
- Consider these questions when choosing a financial advisor:
  - Which one do you trust the most?
  - Which one is the most competent?
  - Which one will you enjoy interacting with the most?
  - Use your best judgement without fear, and hopefully you'll enjoy a long-term, successful relationship.

- Once you make a decision on a financial advisor, listen closely and heed their advice. They are experts in their craft and will always look out for your best interest. They're usually worth exponentially more than their fee. However, you will need to maintain great faith throughout your relationship with them, especially during the days of market volatility.
- Financial advisors do not predict short-term market swings. They don't know what is going to happen in the market tomorrow or any day after. They provide you with assistance in achieving your long-term financial and life goals.
- The financial advisor's fee should be fair and in line with the marketplace. Cover this at the beginning of your relationship. Then, put the fee out of your mind and focus all your efforts on the process to reach your financial and life goals.

Chapter Four: Creating Wealth

- Creating wealth is simple: spend less than what you earn.
- You can start small by dollar-cost-averaging into your 401(k), IRA, Roth, or investment account. Just get started and you'll be amazed at how quickly these investments build up. You must deny yourself the use of these funds today to reap the rewards of their future purpose.

- Be industrious. Don't be afraid to start a business or aggressively climb the corporate ladder by taking on additional responsibility. Also, don't be afraid to invest your money in stocks and real estate. Let your value system guide you to make smart choices with these vital aspects of your life. As they say, shoot for the moon, and if you miss, you will be with the stars.
- Make sure you invest a large portion of your money in growth. Equities and real estate are good options.
- If you have kids or grandkids, consider starting a 529 investment program for their future education. Educating these treasures of your life may turn out to be the best investment you make.
- If your child or grandchild has income, consider starting and funding a Roth for them. Most likely, they're not yet capable of supporting such an investment, but it will surely serve as great financial vehicle for them in the future. If possible, consider funding their ROTH until they're able to do it on their own.
- If you don't know how to invest in the various markets, choose a competent financial advisor. This person should be able to properly educate you, assist you, or make all investments for you. Yes, I'm biased in my opinion, but this could be one of the best financial decisions of your lifetime.
- Remember, a successful investor is one who reaches their long-term financial goals. Follow the six time-

tested principles of investing for your best chance of success:

 - **Trust:** Have faith in the future and be optimistic.
 - **Patience:** Live with a peaceful heart.
 - **Discipline:** Take plenty of time to determine your goals and set an appropriate course to reach them.
 - **Asset Allocation:** Where you have your money is the return you will get.
 - **Diversification:** A pact with heaven, not making a killing and not getting killed.
 - **Rebalancing:** Keep your strategy in place for the long term.

Chapter Five: Managing and Protecting Wealth

- Reread the tale of two investments: bonds versus growing dividend stocks. The long-term difference is a life-changer and a central concept to understanding the great opportunity before you.
- Protecting wealth has more to do with protecting your future purchasing power than keeping your long-term investments stable. If you don't fully understand this concept, have a competent financial advisor take care of it for you.
- Taxes must be considered when structuring your investment portfolio because they erode your pool of money.

- The primary job of a competent financial advisor is to protect you from yourself. Your emotions are most likely your worst enemy when considering your long-term investment goals.
- A strategically positioned portfolio of individual equities, mutual funds, or exchange traded funds (either passive or managed), backed by a Monte Carlo-based financial plan that establishes a personal financial policy statement will help you achieve your financial goals. A competent financial advisor can do this work for you and most importantly keep you on track for your entire life.
- Life insurance is an important tool to leverage your estate and protect your family with the proper resources if something tragic were to happen to you. Seek competent advice before buying any life insurance policy because different policies exist to suit people with different needs. For instance, the type of life insurance policy for a young couple with young children is most likely much different than one that's good for an older person with a substantial business interest.

Chapter Six: Building a Legacy

- Legacy planning is about more than just finances. There is a spiritual side to it as well. Think about the saints of the past and their legacy of charitable service and faith in our Lord. Many were martyred for their religious beliefs.

- Believe it or not, legacy planning is most likely within your value system. If you wrote down your value system, go back and take a look.
- The fork in the road: Spend the last dollar at your death? Or create an enduring legacy pool of wealth for your kids and charities, not only for today but for the foreseeable future? Which option do you associate with greed?
- Long-term care insurance—another fork in the road: I will take care of my own financial needs in my old age or buy insurance to cover this expense and leverage my investments to the kids and charity. Or I will let the taxpayers take care of my final health care expenses. Hmm...it seems like something here would be covered in your value system you thoughtfully put on paper (now laminated and in your back pocket). Now might be a good time to take a look.
- Think about tithing during your lifetime and perhaps tithing your final estate.
- Consider setting up a charitable trust or donor advised fund (DAF) with your financial team (financial advisor, estate attorney, and CPA). Not only is this a wonderful way to extend your legacy far beyond your years on Earth, but it's also a great way to introduce your children to the concept of charitable giving.
- Just about everyone needs a last will and testament,

power of attorney, and power of health. A caring and competent estate attorney will guide you through all of this and exactly what else might be needed for your particular situation.

It's All about Faith

You've probably noticed one central theme to the entire content of this book is faith. It has a role in choosing an advisor, creating wealth, protecting wealth, and leaving a legacy. Truthfully, faith has a role in everything.

Remember the story of Jesus when he went back to his hometown. Very few miracles occurred while he was there because the people saw him only as a carpenter and not as the Son of God. They lacked faith, and consequently, they lacked miracles.

Miracles cannot happen without faith. My advice to all who read this is to have faith in the future, be present in the moment, and live your life in a peaceful manner. Live with those altruistic intentions and have the discipline to plan wisely. Then, you will have set forth a soulfully rich and sweepingly successful course for the future.

My adoptive parents took me in as an infant and gave me every ounce of love they had to give. They instilled in me high moral values and a deep understanding of faith. That initial act of love has extended far beyond my childhood and into my adult life. I've been able to create a successful career, have a beautiful family, and help numerous clients achieve purposeful wealth and leave a strong legacy. You can do all that too. The key is faith. Once you have it, anything is possible.

Reader Notes

Thank you so much for reading my words about building and managing wealth and living in faith. We are all children of God and deserve to live in a world of peace, love, and prosperity. I hope you have a very happy life and have benefited from reading this. May God bless your eternal soul.

Please take some time to write some of the most important lessons you've learned from these pages, and perhaps future generations can benefit from your words as well.

Appendix 1

Financial Goal Plan

Financial Goal Plan

Matthew and Mary Client

March 20, 2018

Prepared by:

Mark Aho

Raymond James
205 N. Lakeshore Blvd
Suite B
Marquette, MI 49855
(906) 226-0880 | MARK.AHO@RAYMONDJAMES.COM
http://markahofinancial.com

Securities offered through Raymond James Financial Services, Inc., member FINRA/SIPC. Investment Advisory Services offered through Raymond James Financial Services Advisors, Inc. and/or the Independent Registered Investment Advisor, or both. Please refer to your advisory services contract and form ADV for more information. Your financial advisor may operate under a separate business entity. The business entity is independent of Raymond James Financial Services and is not a broker/dealer. Raymond James is not affiliated with any other entities listed herein.

Table Of Contents

IMPORTANT DISCLOSURE INFORMATION

IMPORTANT: The projections or other information generated by Goal Planning & Monitoring regarding the likelihood of various investment outcomes are hypothetical in nature, do not reflect actual investment results, and are not guarantees of future results.

The return assumptions in Goal Planning & Monitoring are not reflective of any specific product, and do not include any fees or expenses that may be incurred by investing in specific products. The actual returns of a specific product may be more or less than the returns used in Goal Planning & Monitoring. It is not possible to directly invest in an index. Financial forecasts, rates of return, risk, inflation, and other assumptions may be used as the basis for illustrations. They should not be considered a guarantee of future performance or a guarantee of achieving overall financial objectives. Past performance is not a guarantee or a predictor of future results of either the indices or any particular investment.

Goal Planning & Monitoring results may vary with each use and over time.

Goal Planning & Monitoring Assumptions and Limitations

Information Provided by You

Information that you provided about your assets, financial goals, and personal situation are key assumptions for the calculations and projections in this Report. Please review the Report sections titled "Personal Information and Summary of Financial Goals", "Current Portfolio Allocation", and "Tax and Inflation Options" to verify the accuracy of these assumptions. If any of the assumptions are incorrect, you should notify your financial advisor. Even small changes in assumptions can have a substantial impact on the results shown in this Report. The information provided by you should be reviewed periodically and updated when either the information or your circumstances change.

All asset and net worth information included in this Report was provided by you or your designated agents, and is not a substitute for the information contained in the official account statements provided to you by custodians. The current asset data and values contained in those account statements should be used to update the asset information included in this Report, as necessary.

Assumptions and Limitations

Goal Planning & Monitoring offers several methods of calculating results, each of which provides one outcome from a wide range of possible outcomes. All results in this Report are hypothetical in nature, do not reflect actual investment results, and are not guarantees of future results. All results use simplifying assumptions that do not completely or accurately reflect your specific circumstances. No Plan or Report has the ability to accurately predict the future. As investment returns, inflation, taxes, and other economic conditions vary from the Goal Planning & Monitoring assumptions, your actual results will vary (perhaps significantly) from those presented in this Report.

All Goal Planning & Monitoring calculations use asset class returns, not returns of actual investments. The average annual historical returns are calculated using the indices contained in this Report, which serve as proxies for their respective asset classes. The index data are for the period 1970 - 2010. The portfolio returns are calculated by weighting individual return assumptions for each asset class according to your portfolio allocation. The portfolio returns may have been modified by including adjustments to the total return and the inflation rate. The portfolio returns assume reinvestment of interest and dividends at net asset value without taxes, and also assume that the portfolio has been rebalanced to reflect the initial recommendation. No portfolio rebalancing costs, including taxes, if applicable, are deducted from the portfolio value. No portfolio allocation eliminates risk or guarantees investment results.

Goal Planning & Monitoring does not provide recommendations for any products or securities.

IMPORTANT DISCLOSURE INFORMATION

Asset Class Name	Projected Return Assumption	Projected Standard Deviation
Cash & Cash Alternatives	1.00%	2.00%
Investment Grade Long Maturity Fixed Income	4.45%	9.63%
Investment Grade Intermediate Maturity Fixed Inc	4.40%	5.27%
Investment Grade Short Maturity Fixed Income	4.14%	4.49%
Non-Investment Grade Fixed Income	5.86%	10.01%
Non-U.S. Fixed Income	3.63%	9.88%
Global Fixed Income Strategies	4.02%	6.52%
Multi-Sector Fixed Income Strategies	5.12%	4.79%
Fixed Income Other	4.26%	4.98%
U.S. Large Cap Blend	6.84%	18.06%
U.S. Large Cap Value	6.84%	18.06%
U.S. Large Cap Growth	6.84%	18.06%
U.S. Mid Cap Equity	7.07%	19.64%
U.S. Small Cap Equity	7.29%	22.15%
Non-U.S. Developed Market Equity	7.11%	20.46%
Non-U.S. Emerging Market Equity	8.21%	26.37%
Global Equity Strategies	7.15%	18.85%
Equity Sector Strategies	6.84%	18.06%
Real Estate	6.72%	21.20%
Equity Other	6.82%	19.92%
Alternative Strategies	5.26%	7.25%
Commodities	3.90%	17.23%
Private Market Strategies	9.83%	24.42%
Allocation Strategies (Equity Weighted)	6.15%	12.86%

Asset Class Name	Projected Return Assumption	Projected Standard Deviation
Allocation Strategies (Fixed Income Weighted)	5.16%	8.46%
World Allocation Strategies	6.35%	9.97%
Conservative Strategies	5.16%	7.06%
Moderate Conservative Strategies	5.71%	10.27%
Moderate Strategies	6.14%	13.21%
Moderate Aggressive Strategies	6.84%	17.78%

IMPORTANT DISCLOSURE INFORMATION

Risks Inherent in Investing

Investing in fixed income securities involves interest rate risk, credit risk, and inflation risk. Interest rate risk is the possibility that bond prices will decrease because of an interest rate increase. When interest rates rise, bond prices and the values of fixed income securities fall. When interest rates fall, bond prices and the values of fixed income securities rise. Credit risk is the risk that a company will not be able to pay its debts, including the interest on its bonds. This risk is higher with non-investment grade fixed income securities. Inflation risk is the possibility that the interest paid on an investment in bonds will be lower than the inflation rate, decreasing purchasing power.

Cash alternatives typically include money market securities and U.S. treasury bills. Investing in such cash alternatives involves inflation risk. In addition, investments in money market securities may involve credit risk and a risk of principal loss. Because money market securities are neither insured nor guaranteed by the Federal Deposit Insurance Corporation or any other government agency, there is no guarantee the value of your investment will be maintained at $1.00 per share. U.S. Treasury bills are subject to market risk if sold prior to maturity. Market risk is the possibility that the value, when sold, might be less than the purchase price.

Investing in stock securities involves volatility risk, market risk, business risk, and industry risk. The prices of most stocks fluctuate. Volatility risk is the chance that the value of a stock will fall. Market risk is chance that the prices of all stocks will fall due to conditions in the economic environment. Business risk is the chance that a specific company's stock will fall because of issues affecting it. Industry risk is the chance that a set of factors particular to an industry group will adversely affect stock prices within the industry. (See "Asset Class – Stocks" in the Glossary section of this Important Disclosure Information for a summary of the relative potential volatility of different types of stocks.)

International investing involves additional risks including, but not limited to, changes in currency exchange rates, differences in accounting and taxation policies, and political or economic instabilities that can increase or decrease returns.

Commodities are generally considered speculative because of the significant potential for investment loss. Commodities are volatile investments and should only form a small part of a diversified portfolio. There may be sharp price fluctuations even during periods when prices overall are rising.

Report Is a Snapshot and Does Not Provide Legal, Tax, or Accounting Advice

This Report provides a snapshot of your current financial position and can help you to focus on your financial resources and goals, and to create a plan of action. Because the results are calculated over many years, small changes can create large differences in future results. You should use this Report to help you focus on the factors that are most important to you. This Report does not provide legal, tax, or accounting advice. Before making decisions with legal, tax, or accounting ramifications, you should consult appropriate professionals for advice that is specific to your situation.

This information is provided for your convenience, but should not be used as a substitute for your account's monthly statements and trade confirmations. It has been gathered from information provided by you and other sources believed to be reliable.

Goal Planning & Monitoring Methodology

Goal Planning & Monitoring offers several methods of calculating results, each of which provides one outcome from a wide range of possible outcomes. The methods used are: "Average Returns," "Bad Timing," "Class Sensitivity," and "Monte Carlo Simulations."

Results Using Average Returns

The Results Using Average Returns are calculated using one average return for your pre-retirement period and one average return for your post-retirement period. Average Returns are a simplifying assumption. In the real world, investment returns can (and often do) vary widely from year to year and vary widely from a long-term average return.

Results with Bad Timing

Results with Bad Timing are calculated by using low returns in one or two years, and average returns for all remaining years of the Plan. For most Plans, the worst time for low returns is when you begin taking substantial withdrawals from your portfolio. The Results with Bad Timing assume that you earn a low return in the year(s) you select and then an Adjusted Average Return in all other years. This Adjusted Average Return is calculated so that the average return of the Results with Bad Timing is equal to the return(s) used in calculating the Results Using Average Returns. This allows you to compare two results with the same overall average return, where one (the Results with Bad Timing) has low returns in one or two years.

The default for the first year of low returns is two standard deviations less than the average return, and the default for the second year is one standard deviation less than the average return.

IMPORTANT DISCLOSURE INFORMATION

Results Using Class Sensitivity

The Results Using Class Sensitivity are calculated by using different return assumptions for one or more asset classes during the years you select. These results show how your Plan would be affected if the annual returns for one or more asset classes were different than the average returns for a specified period in your Plan.

Results Using Monte Carlo Simulations

Monte Carlo simulations are used to show how variations in rates of return each year can affect your results. A Monte Carlo simulation calculates the results of your Plan by running it many times, each time using a different sequence of returns. Some sequences of returns will give you better results, and some will give you worse results. These multiple trials provide a range of possible results, some successful (you would have met all your goals) and some unsuccessful (you would not have met all your goals). The percentage of trials that were successful is the probability that your Plan, with all its underlying assumptions, could be successful. In Goal Planning & Monitoring, this is the Probability of Success. Analogously, the percentage of trials that were unsuccessful is the Probability of Failure. The Results Using Monte Carlo Simulations indicate the likelihood that an event may occur as well as the likelihood that it may not occur. In analyzing this information, please note that the analysis does not take into account actual market conditions, which may severely affect the outcome of your goals over the long-term.

Goal Planning & Monitoring Presentation of Results

The Results Using Average Returns, Bad Timing, and Class Sensitivity display the results using an "Estimated % of Goal Funded" and a "Safety Margin."

Estimated % of Goal Funded

For each Goal, the "Estimated % of Goal Funded" is the sum of the assets used to fund the Goal divided by the sum of the Goal's expenses. All values are in current dollars. A result of 100% or more does not guarantee that you will reach a Goal, nor does a result under 100% guarantee that you will not. Rather, this information is meant to identify possible shortfalls in this Plan, and is not a guarantee that a certain percentage of your Goals will be funded. The percentage reflects a projection of the total cost of the Goal that was actually funded based upon all the assumptions that are included in this Plan, and assumes that you execute all aspects of the Plan as you have indicated.

Safety Margin

The Safety Margin is the estimated value of your assets at the end of this Plan, based on all the assumptions included in this Report. Only you can determine if that Safety Margin is sufficient for your needs.

Bear Market Loss and Bear Market Test

The Bear Market Loss shows how a portfolio would have been impacted during the worst bear market since the Great Depression. Depending on the composition of the portfolio, the worst bear market is either the "Great Recession" or the "Bond Bear Market."

The Great Recession, from November 2007 through February 2009, was the worst bear market for stocks since the Great Depression. In Goal Planning & Monitoring, the Great Recession Return is the rate of return, during the Great Recession, for a portfolio comprised of cash, bonds, stocks, and alternatives, with an asset mix equivalent to the portfolio referenced.

The Bond Bear Market, from July 1979 through February 1980, was the worst bear market for bonds since the Great Depression. In Goal Planning & Monitoring, the Bond Bear Market Return is the rate of return, for the Bond Bear Market period, for a portfolio comprised of cash, bonds, stocks, and alternatives, with an asset mix equivalent to the portfolio referenced.

The Bear Market Loss shows: 1) either the Great Recession Return or the Bond Bear Market Return, whichever is lower, and 2) the potential loss, if you had been invested in this cash-bond-stock-alternative portfolio during the period with the lower return. In general, most portfolios with a stock allocation of 20% or more have a lower Great Recession Return, and most portfolios with a combined cash and bond allocation of 80% or more have a lower Bond Bear Market Return.

The Bear Market Test, included in the Stress Tests, examines the impact on your Plan results if an identical Great Recession or Bond Bear Market, whichever would be worse, occurred this year. The Bear Market Test shows the likelihood that you could fund your Needs, Wants and Wishes after experiencing such an event.

IMPORTANT DISCLOSURE INFORMATION

Even though you are using projected returns for all other Goal Planning & Monitoring results, the Bear Market Loss and Bear Market Test use returns calculated from historical indices. These results are calculated using only three asset classes – Cash, Bonds, and Stocks. Alternative asset classes (e.g., real estate, commodities) are included in the Stocks asset class. The indices and the resulting returns for the Great Recession and the Bond Bear Market are:

Asset Class	Index	Great Recession Return 11/2007 – 02/2009	Bond Bear Market Return 07/1979 – 02/1980
Cash	Ibbotson U.S. 30-day Treasury Bills	2.31%	7.08%
Bond	Ibbotson Intermediate-Term Government Bonds – Total Return	15.61%	-8.89%
Stock	S&P 500 - Total Return	-50.95%	14.61%
Alternative	HFRI FOF: Diversified*	-19.87%	N/A
	S&P GSCI Commodity - Total Return**	N/A	23.21%

*Hedge Fund Research Indices Fund of Funds

**S&P GSCI was formerly the Goldman Sachs Commodity Index

Because the Bear Market Loss and Bear Market Test use the returns from asset class indices rather than the returns of actual investments, they do not represent the performance for any specific portfolio, and are not a guarantee of minimum or maximum levels of losses or gains for any portfolio. The actual performance of your portfolio may differ substantially from those shown in the Great Recession Return, the Bond Bear Market Return, the Bear Market Loss, and the Bear Market Test.

Goal Planning & Monitoring Risk Assessment

The Goal Planning & Monitoring Risk Assessment highlights some – but not all – of the trade-offs you might consider when deciding how to invest your money. This approach does not provide a comprehensive, psychometrically-based, or scientifically-validated profile of your risk tolerance, loss tolerance, or risk capacity, and is provided for informational purposes only.

Goal Planning & Monitoring uses your risk score to select a risk-based portfolio on the Target Band page. This risk-based portfolio selection is provided for informational purposes only, and you should consider it to be a starting point for conversations with your advisor. It is your responsibility to select the Target Portfolio you want Goal Planning & Monitoring to use. The selection of your Target Portfolio, and other investment decisions, should be made by you, after discussions with your advisor and, if needed, other financial and/or legal professionals.

Net Worth Detail - All Resources

This is your Net Worth Detail as of 03/20/2018. Your Net Worth is the difference between what you own (your Assets) and what you owe (your Liabilities). To get an accurate Net Worth statement, make certain all of your Assets and Liabilities are entered

Description	Matthew	Mary	Joint	Total
Investment Assets				
Employer Retirement Plans				
401(k)	$150,000			$150,000
401(k)		$150,000		$150,000
Taxable and/or Tax-Free Accounts				
Investment Account			$50,000	$50,000
Total Investment Assets:	**$150,000**	**$150,000**	**$50,000**	**$350,000**
Other Assets				
Home and Personal Assets				
Personal Property			$50,000	$50,000
Personal Residence			$235,000	$235,000
Total Other Assets:	**$0**	**$0**	**$285,000**	**$285,000**
Liabilities				
Personal Real Estate Loan:				
Personal Residence			$135,000	$135,000
Total Liabilities:	**$0**	**$0**	**$135,000**	**$135,000**
Net Worth:				**$500,000**

See Important Disclosure Information section in this Report for explanations of assumptions, limitations, methodologies, and a glossary.

Net Worth Summary - All Resources

This is your Net Worth Summary as of 03/20/2018. Your Net Worth is the difference between what you own (your Assets) and what you owe (your Liabilities). To get an accurate Net Worth statement, make certain all of your Assets and Liabilities are entered.

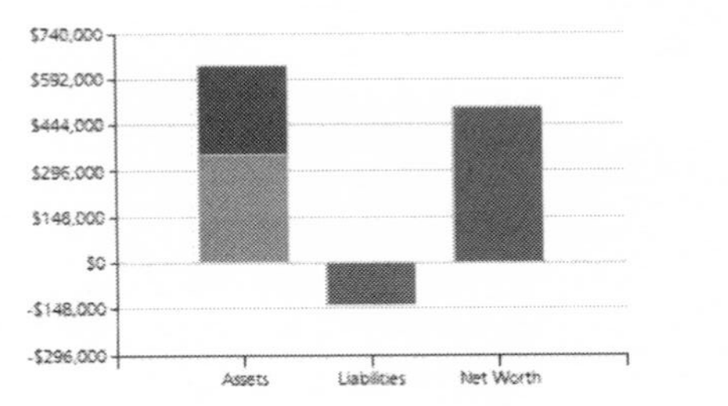

Investment Assets		$350,000
Other Assets	+	$285,000
Total Assets		$635,000
Total Liabilities	-	$135,000
Net Worth		$500,000

Description	Total
Investment Assets	
Employer Retirement Plans	$300,000
Taxable and/or Tax-Free Accounts	$50,000
Total Investment Assets:	**$350,000**
Other Assets	
Home and Personal Assets	$285,000
Total Other Assets:	**$285,000**
Liabilities	
Personal Real Estate Loan:	$135,000
Total Liabilities:	**$135,000**
Net Worth:	**$500,000**

See Important Disclosure Information section in this Report for explanations of assumptions, limitations, methodologies, and a glossary.

Prepared for : Matthew and Mary Client   Company: Raymond James   Prepared by: Mark Aho

03/20/2018   Page 7 of 29

Current Portfolio Allocation

This page shows how your Investment Assets are currently allocated among the different Asset Classes. It includes only those Assets you have identified to fund Goals in this Plan.

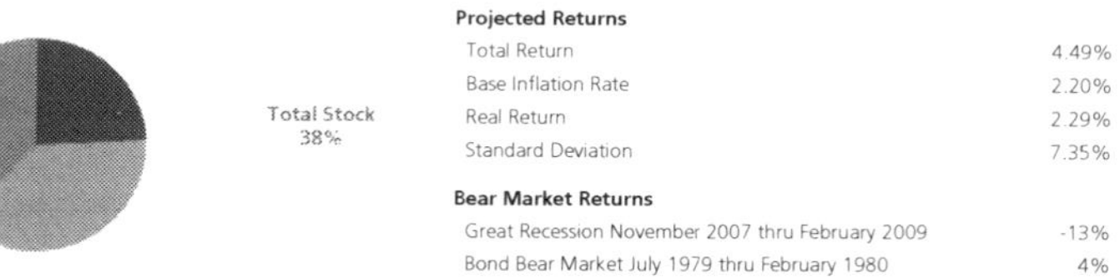

Projected Returns

Total Return	4.49%
Base Inflation Rate	2.20%
Real Return	2.29%
Standard Deviation	7.35%

Bear Market Returns

Great Recession November 2007 thru February 2009	-13%
Bond Bear Market July 1979 thru February 1980	4%

Asset Class	Rate of Return	Investment Portfolio	
		Value	% of Total
Cash & Cash Alternatives	1.00%	$85,000	24.29%
Investment Grade Intermediate Maturity Fixed Inc	4.40%	$132,500	37.86%
U.S. Large Cap Blend	6.84%	$132,500	37.86%
	Total :	**$350,000**	**100%**

See Important Disclosure Information section in this Report for explanations of assumptions, limitations, methodologies, and a glossary.

Risk Assessment

You chose a Risk Score of 60.

Appropriate Portfolio: Balanced w/ Growth
Percentage Stock: 78.00%
Average Return: 6.43%

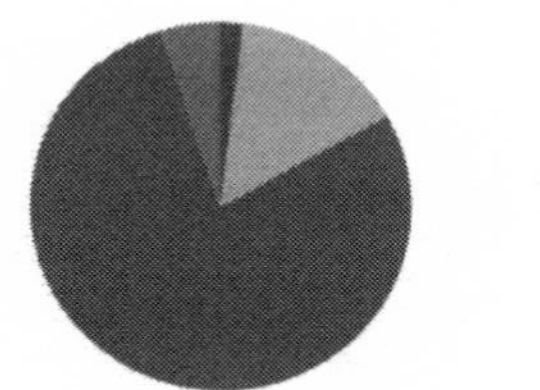

Great Recession Return Loss for this Portfolio

If this loss would cause you to sell your investments, you should select a lower score. Don't go past your Breaking Point.

During the Great Recession Return (November 2007 - February 2009) this portfolio had a loss of:

-38%

If you invest $350,000 in this portfolio and the same loss occurred again, you would lose:

-$134,214

See Important Disclosure Information section in this Report for explanations of assumptions, limitations, methodologies, and a glossary.

Prepared for : Matthew and Mary Client | Company: Raymond James | Prepared by: Mark Aho
03/20/2018 | Page 9 of 29

Portfolio Table

The Risk-Based Portfolio was selected from this list of Portfolios, based upon the risk assessment. The Target Band is comprised of the portfolio(s) that could be appropriate for you, based upon the Risk-Based Portfolio indicated. The Target Portfolio was selected by you. The Average Real Return is equal to the Average Total Return minus the inflation rate of 2.20%. Refer to the Standard Deviation column in the chart below to compare the relative risk of your Current Portfolio to the Target Portfolio.

Current	Risk Based	Target Band	Name	Cash	Bond	Stock	Alternative	Average Return Total	Average Return Real	Standard Deviation
→			Current	24.29%	37.86%	37.86%	0.00%	4.49%	2.29%	7.35%
			Conservative	2.00%	71.00%	27.00%	0.00%	5.10%	2.90%	6.54%
			Conservative Balanced	2.00%	51.00%	47.00%	0.00%	5.60%	3.40%	9.41%
			Balanced	2.00%	31.00%	64.00%	3.00%	6.10%	3.90%	12.31%
	→		Balanced w/ Growth	2.00%	15.00%	78.00%	5.00%	6.43%	4.23%	14.57%
		→	(c) New Allocation	0.00%	13.00%	87.00%	0.00%	6.74%	4.54%	16.59%
			Growth	2.00%	0.00%	93.00%	5.00%	6.83%	4.63%	17.21%

(c) This is a Custom Portfolio created only for your plan and the name is for identification purposes only.

Return vs. Risk Graph

When deciding how to invest your money, you must determine the amount of risk you are willing to assume to pursue a desired return. The Return versus Risk Graph reflects a set of portfolios that assume a low relative level of risk for each level of return, or conversely an optimal return for the degree of investment risk taken. The graph also shows the position of the Current, Target, Risk-Based, and Custom Portfolios. The positioning of these portfolios illustrates how their respective risks and returns compare to each other as well as the optimized level of risk and return represented by the Portfolios.

This graph shows the relationship of return and risk for each Portfolio in the chart above.

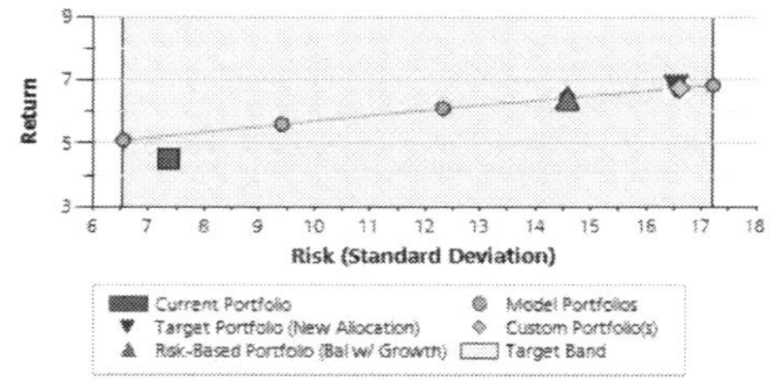

See Important Disclosure Information section in this Report for explanations of assumptions, limitations, methodologies, and a glossary.

Prepared for : Matthew and Mary Client　　Company: Raymond James　　Prepared by: Mark Aho

03/20/2018　　Page 10 of 29

What If Worksheet

This Worksheet allows you to analyze and compare the results of one or more scenarios that you created by varying the Plan assumptions.

Goals	Estimated % of Goal Funded			
	Current Scenario		What If 1	
	Average Return	Bad Timing	Average Return	Bad Timing
Needs	62%	60%	100%	100%
10 Retirement				
10 Health Care				
Wants	0%	0%	100%	100%
5 Travel				
Safety Margin (Value at End of Plan)				
Current dollars (in thousands) :	$0	$0	$1,430	$778
Future dollars (in thousands) :	$0	$0	$3,645	$1,984

Monte Carlo Results	Likelihood of Funding All Goals	
Your Confidence Zone: 75% - 90%	0% Probability of Success Below Confidence Zone	85% Probability of Success In Confidence Zone
Total Spending :	$2,907,559	$2,424,100

* Indicates different data between the Scenario in the first column and the Scenario in any other column.

See Important Disclosure Information section in this Report for explanations of assumptions, limitations, methodologies, and a glossary.

What If Worksheet

Key Assumptions	Current Scenario		What If 1
Stress Tests			
Method(s)	Bad Timing Program Estimate Years of bad returns: 2032: -10.21% 2033: -2.86%		Bad Timing Program Estimate Years of bad returns: 2037: -26.45% 2038: -9.85%
Funding Order			
Assets - Ignore Earmarks	No		No
Retirement Income - Ignore Earmarks	No		No
Hypothetical Average Rate of Return			
Before Retirement :	Current	*	New Allocation
Total Return :	4.49%	*	6.74%
Standard Deviation :	7.35%	*	16.59%
Total Return Adjustment :	0.00%		0.00%
Adjusted Real Return :	2.29%	*	4.54%
After Retirement :	Current	*	New Allocation
Total Return :	4.49%	*	6.74%
Standard Deviation :	7.35%	*	16.59%
Total Return Adjustment :	0.00%		0.00%
Adjusted Real Return :	2.29%	*	4.54%
Base inflation rate :	2.20%		2.20%
Tax-Free Options			
Before Retirement			
Reallocate a portion of bonds to tax-free:	No		No
Percent of bond allocation to treat as tax-free:	0.00%		0.00%
After Retirement			
Reallocate a portion of bonds to tax-free:	No		No
Percent of bond allocation to treat as tax-free:	0.00%		0.00%

* indicates different data between the Scenario in the first column and the Scenario in any other column.

See Important Disclosure Information section in this Report for explanations of assumptions, limitations, methodologies, and a glossary.

What If Worksheet

Key Assumptions	Current Scenario		What If 1
Goals			
Living Expense			
Retirement Age			
Matthew	65	*	70
Mary	65	*	70
Planning Age			
Matthew	91		91
Mary	93		93
One Retired			
Matthew Retired and Mary Employed	$36,000		$36,000
Mary Retired and Matthew Employed	$48,000		$48,000
Both Retired			
Both Retired	$84,000		$84,000
One Alone - Retired			
Mary Alone Retired	$67,200		$67,200
Matthew Alone Retired	$72,000		$72,000
One Alone - Employed			
Matthew Alone Employed	$48,000		$48,000
Mary Alone Employed	$36,000		$36,000
Health Care			
Percentage to increase costs :	100%		100%
Cost determined by Schedule :	See details		See details
Travel			
Year :	2032	*	2037
Cost :	$10,000		$10,000
Is recurring :	Yes		Yes
Years between occurrences :	1		1
Number of occurrences :	15		15

* Indicates different data between the Scenario in the first column and the Scenario in any other column.

See Important Disclosure Information section in this Report for explanations of assumptions, limitations, methodologies, and a glossary.

What If Worksheet

Key Assumptions	Current Scenario		What If 1
Retirement Income			
Social Security			
Select Social Security Strategy	At FRA	*	At Age 70
Matthew			
Filing Method :	Normal		Normal
Age to File Application :	67	*	70
Age Retirement Benefits begin :	67	*	70
First Year Benefit :	$24,665	*	$31,580
Mary			
Filing Method :	Normal		Normal
Age to File Application :	67	*	70
Age Retirement Benefits begin :	67	*	70
First Year Benefit :	$26,086	*	$33,413
Reduce Benefits By :	0%		0%
Asset Additions			
401(k)	3.00%	*	16.00%
Roth:	0.00%		0.00%
Maximum contribution each year:	No		No
% Designated as Roth:	0.00%		0.00%
Plan addition amount:	$2,009	*	$10,595
Year additions begin:	2018		2018
Matthew - Fund All Goals			
401(k)	3.00%	*	16.00%
Roth:	0.00%		0.00%
Maximum contribution each year:	No		No
% Designated as Roth:	0.00%		0.00%
Plan addition amount:	$2,163	*	$11,326
Year additions begin:	2018		2018
Mary - Fund All Goals			

* indicates different data between the Scenario in the first column and the Scenario in any other column.

See Important Disclosure Information section in this Report for explanations of assumptions, limitations, methodologies, and a glossary.

What If Worksheet

Key Assumptions	Current Scenario	What If 1
Extra Savings by Tax Category		
Matthew's Qualified		$0
Mary's Qualified		$0
Matthew's Roth		$0
Mary's Roth		$0
Matthew's Tax-Deferred		$0
Mary's Tax-Deferred		$0
Taxable		$0
Tax Options		
Include Tax Penalties :	Yes	Yes
Change Tax Rate?	No	No
Year To Change :		
Change Tax Rate by this % (+ or -) :	0.00%	0.00%

* Indicates different data between the Scenario in the first column and the Scenario in any other column.

See Important Disclosure Information section in this Report for explanations of assumptions, limitations, methodologies, and a glossary.

Worksheet Detail - Combined Details

Scenario : What If 1 with Bad Timing

These pages provide a picture of how your Investment Portfolio may hypothetically perform over the life of this Plan. The graph shows the effect on the value of your Investment Portfolio for each year. The chart shows the detailed activities that increase and decrease your Investment Portfolio value each year including the funds needed to pay for each of your Goals. Shortfalls that occur in a particular year are denoted with an 'X' under the Goal column.

Total Portfolio Value Graph

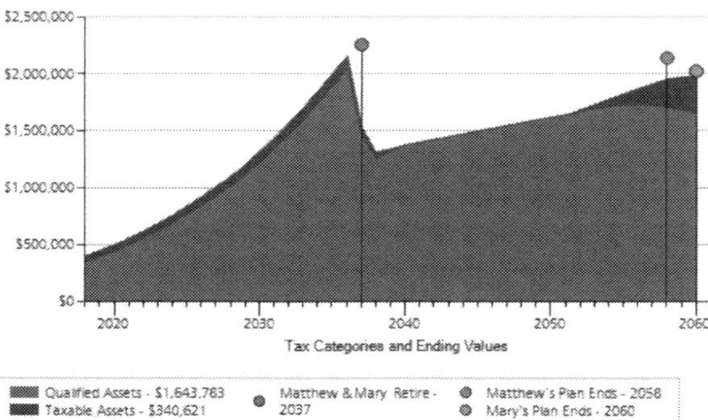

x - denotes shortfall

See Important Disclosure Information section in this Report for explanations of assumptions, limitations, methodologies, and a glossary.

Worksheet Detail - Combined Details

Scenario : What If 1 with Bad Timing

Event or Ages	Year	Beginning Portfolio Value		Additions To Assets	Other Additions	Post Retirement Income	Investment Earnings	Taxes	Funds Used			Ending Portfolio Value
		Earmarked	Fund All Goals						Retirement	Health Care	Travel	
51 / 51	2018	0	350,000	21,921	0	0	25,067	837	0	0	0	396,151
52 / 52	2019	0	396,151	22,403	0	0	28,211	880	0	0	0	445,885
53 / 53	2020	0	445,885	22,896	0	0	31,596	924	0	0	0	499,452
54 / 54	2021	0	499,452	23,400	0	0	35,240	971	0	0	0	557,121
55 / 55	2022	0	557,121	23,915	0	0	39,162	1,020	0	0	0	619,177
56 / 56	2023	0	619,177	24,441	0	0	43,380	1,072	0	0	0	685,925
57 / 57	2024	0	685,925	24,978	0	0	47,915	1,126	0	0	0	757,692
58 / 58	2025	0	757,692	25,528	0	0	52,789	1,183	0	0	0	834,825
59 / 59	2026	0	834,825	26,089	0	0	58,026	1,243	0	0	0	917,697
60 / 60	2027	0	917,697	26,663	0	0	63,650	1,306	0	0	0	1,006,704
61 / 61	2028	0	1,006,704	27,250	0	0	69,688	1,373	0	0	0	1,102,270
62 / 62	2029	0	1,102,270	27,849	0	0	76,170	1,442	0	0	0	1,204,847
63 / 63	2030	0	1,204,847	28,462	0	0	83,125	1,515	0	0	0	1,314,919
64 / 64	2031	0	1,314,919	29,089	0	0	90,586	1,592	0	0	0	1,433,002
65 / 65	2032	0	1,433,002	29,728	0	0	98,588	1,673	0	0	0	1,559,646
66 / 66	2033	0	1,559,646	30,383	0	0	107,168	1,757	0	0	0	1,695,439
67 / 67	2034	0	1,695,439	31,051	0	0	116,365	1,846	0	0	0	1,841,009
68 / 68	2035	0	1,841,009	31,734	0	0	126,223	1,940	0	0	0	1,997,026
69 / 69	2036	0	1,997,026	32,432	0	0	136,785	2,038	0	0	0	2,164,205
Matthew & Mary Retire	2037	0	2,164,205	0	0	98,273	-550,517	19,794	127,012	19,191	15,121	1,530,843
71 / 71	2038	0	1,530,843	0	0	100,435	-142,870	16,675	129,807	19,613	15,453	1,306,860
72 / 72	2039	0	1,306,860	0	0	102,644	113,686	16,229	132,662	20,044	15,793	1,338,461
73 / 73	2040	0	1,338,461	0	0	104,902	116,277	18,171	135,581	20,485	16,141	1,369,262
74 / 74	2041	0	1,369,262	0	0	107,210	118,373	24,905	138,564	20,936	16,496	1,393,946
75 / 75	2042	0	1,393,946	0	0	109,569	120,472	25,452	141,612	21,397	16,859	1,418,667
76 / 76	2043	0	1,418,667	0	0	111,979	122,571	26,012	144,728	21,867	17,229	1,443,381
77 / 77	2044	0	1,443,381	0	0	114,443	124,665	26,585	147,912	22,348	17,609	1,468,035
78 / 78	2045	0	1,468,035	0	0	116,961	126,748	27,170	151,166	22,840	17,996	1,492,573
79 / 79	2046	0	1,492,573	0	0	119,534	128,817	27,767	154,491	23,343	18,392	1,516,930

x - denotes shortfall

See Important Disclosure Information section in this Report for explanations of assumptions, limitations, methodologies, and a glossary.

Prepared for : Matthew and Mary Client — Company: Raymond James — Prepared by: Mark Aho

03/20/2018 — Page 17 of 29

Worksheet Detail - Combined Details

Scenario : What If 1 with Bad Timing

		Beginning Portfolio Value							Funds Used			
Event or Ages	Year	Earmarked	Fund All Goals	Additions To Assets	Other Additions	Post Retirement Income	Investment Earnings	Taxes	Retirement	Health Care	Travel	Ending Portfolio Value
80 / 80	2047	0	1,516,930	0	0	122,164	130,864	28,378	157,890	23,856	18,796	1,541,037
81 / 81	2048	0	1,541,037	0	0	124,851	132,883	29,003	161,364	24,381	19,210	1,564,814
82 / 82	2049	0	1,564,814	0	0	127,598	134,867	29,641	164,914	24,917	19,633	1,588,174
83 / 83	2050	0	1,588,174	0	0	130,405	136,807	30,293	168,542	25,465	20,065	1,611,022
84 / 84	2051	0	1,611,022	0	0	133,274	138,695	30,959	172,250	26,026	20,506	1,633,250
85 / 85	2052	0	1,633,250	0	0	136,206	142,676	29,699	176,039	26,598	0	1,679,795
86 / 86	2053	0	1,679,795	0	0	139,202	146,672	32,178	179,912	27,183	0	1,726,396
87 / 87	2054	0	1,726,396	0	0	142,265	150,660	34,894	183,870	27,782	0	1,772,775
88 / 88	2055	0	1,772,775	0	0	145,395	154,616	37,860	187,915	28,393	0	1,818,617
89 / 89	2056	0	1,818,617	0	0	148,593	158,510	41,087	192,050	29,017	0	1,863,567
90 / 90	2057	0	1,863,567	0	0	151,863	162,342	44,209	196,275	29,656	0	1,907,633
Matthew's Plan Ends	2058	0	1,907,633	0	0	155,203	166,087	47,529	200,593	30,308	0	1,950,493
- / 92	2059	0	1,950,493	0	0	81,546	167,816	51,117	164,005	15,230	0	1,969,503
Mary's Plan Ends	2060	0	1,969,503	0	0	83,340	169,179	54,441	167,613	15,565	0	1,984,404

x - denotes shortfall

See Important Disclosure Information section in this Report for explanations of assumptions, limitations, methodologies, and a glossary.

Worksheet Detail - Combined Details

Scenario : What If 1 with Bad Timing

Notes

- Calculations are based on a "Rolling Year" rather than a Calendar Year. The current date begins the 365-day "Rolling Year".
- Additions and withdrawals occur at the beginning of the year.
- Other Additions come from items entered in the Other Assets section and any applicable proceeds from insurance policies.
- Stock Options and Restricted Stock values are after-tax.
- Strategy Income is based on the particulars of the Goal Strategies selected. Strategy Income from immediate annuities, 72(t) distributions, and variable annuities with a guaranteed minimum withdrawal benefit (GMWB) is pre-tax. Strategy Income from Net Unrealized Appreciation (NUA) is after-tax.
- Post Retirement Income includes the following: Social Security, pension, annuity, rental property, royalty, alimony, part-time employment, trust, and any other retirement income as entered in the Plan.
- When married, if either Social Security Program Estimate or Use a Better Estimate of Annual Benefits is selected for a participant, the program will default to the greater of the selected benefit or the age adjusted spousal benefit, which is based on the other participant's benefit.
- Investment Earnings are calculated on all assets after any withdrawals for 'Goal Expense', 'Taxes on Withdrawals' and 'Tax Penalties' are subtracted.
- The taxes column is a sum of (1) taxes on retirement income, (2) taxes on strategy income, (3) taxes on withdrawals from qualified assets for Required Minimum Distributions, (4) taxes on withdrawals from taxable assets' untaxed gain used to fund Goals in that year, (5) taxes on withdrawals from tax-deferred or qualified assets used to fund goals in that year, and (6) taxes on the investment earnings of taxable assets. Tax rates used are detailed in the Tax and Inflation Options page. (Please note, the Taxes column does not include any taxes owed from the exercise of Stock Options or the vesting of Restricted Stock.)
- Tax Penalties can occur when Qualified and Tax-Deferred Assets are used prior to age 59½. If there is a value in this column, it illustrates that you are using your assets in this Plan in a manner that may incur tax penalties. Generally, it is better to avoid tax penalties whenever possible.
- These calculations do not incorporate penalties associated with use of 529 Plan withdrawals for non-qualified expenses.
- Funds for each Goal Expense are first used from Earmarked Assets. If sufficient funds are not available from Earmarked Assets, Fund All Goals Assets will be used to fund the remaining portion of the Goal Expense, if available in that year.
- All funds needed for a Goal must be available in the year the Goal occurs. Funds from Earmarked Assets that become available after the goal year(s) have passed are not included in the funding of that Goal, and accumulate until the end of the Plan.
- When married, ownership of qualified assets is assumed to roll over to the surviving co-client at the death of the original owner. It is also assumed the surviving co-client inherits all assets of the original owner.
- The Retirement Cash Reserve is the total funding amount for the Cash Reserve at the beginning of each year. The Retirement Cash Reserve is funded from the Earmarked and Fund All Goals columns, and the Cash Reserve amount is included in both the Beginning and Ending Portfolio Values.

x - denotes shortfall

See Important Disclosure Information section in this Report for explanations of assumptions, limitations, methodologies, and a glossary.

Worksheet Detail - Social Security Analysis

Social Security Analysis for What If 1

Social Security Strategy	Selected Strategy	As Soon As Possible	At Retirement	At FRA	At Age 70	Mary begins at age 70 and Matthew begins at FRA
Start age						
Matthew	70	62	70	67	70	67
Mary	70	62	70	67	70	70
First year benefit in current dollars						
Matthew	$31,580	$0	$31,580	$25,468	$31,580	$25,468
Mary	$33,413	$0	$33,413	$26,946	$33,413	$33,413
Total lifetime benefit in current dollars	$1,496,669	$954,962	$1,496,669	$1,364,232	$1,496,669	$1,438,603
Probability of success	85%	65%	85%	75%	85%	81%
Break Even Point						
Matthew	73	N/A	73	67	73	71
Mary	73	N/A	73	67	73	71

See Important Disclosure Information section in this Report for explanations of assumptions, limitations, methodologies, and a glossary.

Worksheet Detail - Social Security Analysis

Social Security Analysis for What If 1

Notes

Selected Strategy:

This is the strategy you selected.

At FRA:

You apply for and begin retirement benefits at your Full Retirement Age (FRA), which is determined by your date of birth. If the retirement age you specified is after your FRA, we assume you will begin benefits at FRA, and we will adjust the benefit for inflation until your retirement age.

At Retirement:

You apply for and begin retirement benefits at the retirement age shown. The benefit is automatically adjusted to account for excess earnings from part-time work and/or taking benefits prior to your FRA, if either is applicable.

As soon as possible:

You apply for and begin benefits at the later of your current age or age 62. The benefit is automatically adjusted to account for excess earnings from part-time work, if applicable, and taking benefits prior to your FRA. If you are age 62 or older, this option is not available.

At age 70:

You apply for and begin benefits at age 70.

(Higher Wage Earner) begins at age 70 and (Lower Wage Earner) begins at FRA:

This strategy is available only if you are married. The higher wage earner applies for and begins benefits at age 70. The lower wage earner applies for and begins benefits at his/her FRA. The higher/lower wage earners are determined based on the employment incomes you specified.

(Higher Wage Earner) files/suspends and (Lower Wage Earner) restricted application:

This strategy is available only if you are married and assumes that you filed for and suspended your benefits prior to April 30, 2016 and your spouse reached age 62 by January 1, 2016. The higher wage earner applies for and suspends taking benefits until age 70. The higher wage earner can file at or after his/her FRA, at which time the spouse (the lower wage earner) files for and takes spousal benefits. The spouse then files for and begins his/her own benefit at age 70, at the higher benefit amount.

The lower wage earner makes a restricted application at his/her FRA. Restricted application allows the account holder to apply only for the "spousal benefit" s/he would be due under dual entitlement rules. At any age beyond his/her FRA, the lower wage earner can apply for and receive benefits based on his/her own work history.

After April 30, 2016, you (or your spouse) can still file and suspend your benefits upon reaching your FRA; but this strategy (that allowed your spouse to receive spousal benefits for the same period that the benefits are suspended) has been discontinued by the Social Security Administration.

(Lower Wage Earner) files/suspends and (Higher Wage Earner) restricted application:

This strategy is available only if you are married and assumes that you filed for and suspended your benefits prior to April 30, 2016 and your spouse reached age 62 by January 1, 2016. The lower wage earner applies for and suspends taking benefits until age 70. The lower wage earner can file at or after his/her FRA, at which time the spouse (the higher wage earner) files for and takes spousal benefits. The spouse then files for and begins his/her own benefit at age 70, at the higher benefit amount.

The higher wage earner makes a restricted application at his/her FRA. Restricted application allows the account holder to apply only for the "spousal benefit" s/he would be due under dual entitlement rules. At any age beyond his/her FRA, the higher wage earner can apply for and receive benefits based on his/her own work history.

After April 30, 2016, you (or your spouse) can still file and suspend your benefits upon reaching your FRA; but this strategy (that allowed your spouse to receive spousal benefits for the same period that the benefits are suspended) has been discontinued by the Social Security Administration.

Maximized Benefits:

This is the strategy that provides the highest estimate of lifetime Social Security income, assuming you live to the age(s) shown on the Detailed Results page.

Total Lifetime Benefit:

The total estimate of benefits you and your co-client, if applicable, would receive in your lifetime, assuming you live to the age(s) shown on the Detailed Results page. This amount is in current (non-inflated) dollars.

Break Even Point:

The age(s) at which this strategy would provide benefits equivalent to the "As Soon As Possible" strategy. If you live longer than the "break even" age for a strategy, your total lifetime benefits using that strategy would be greater than the lifetime benefits of the "As Soon As Possible" strategy. If you are older than age 62 and the "As Soon As Possible" strategy is not shown, the break even comparison uses the strategy that begins at the earliest age(s) as the baseline for comparison.

See Important Disclosure Information section in this Report for explanations of assumptions, limitations, methodologies, and a glossary.

Worksheet Detail - Social Security Combined Details

Social Security Combined Details for What If 1

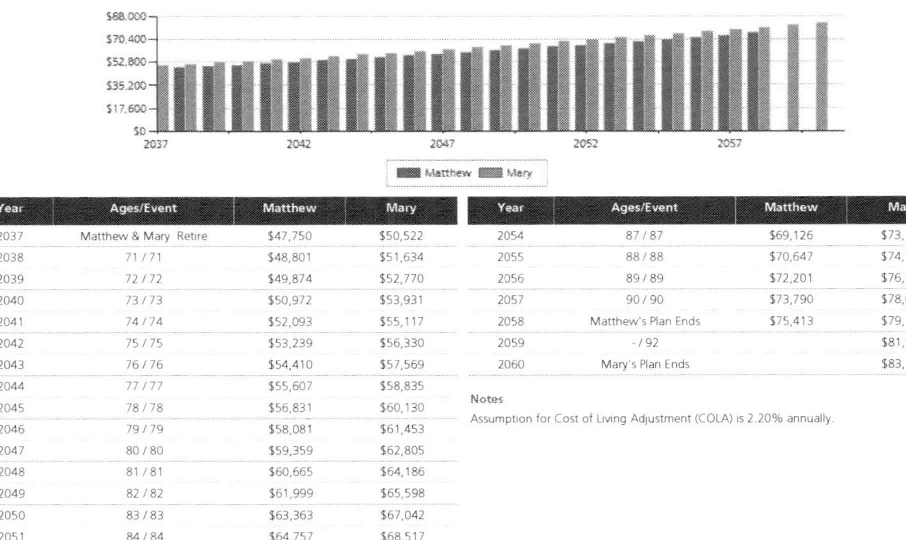

Year	Ages/Event	Matthew	Mary
2037	Matthew & Mary Retire	$47,750	$50,522
2038	71 / 71	$48,801	$51,634
2039	72 / 72	$49,874	$52,770
2040	73 / 73	$50,972	$53,931
2041	74 / 74	$52,093	$55,117
2042	75 / 75	$53,239	$56,330
2043	76 / 76	$54,410	$57,569
2044	77 / 77	$55,607	$58,835
2045	78 / 78	$56,831	$60,130
2046	79 / 79	$58,081	$61,453
2047	80 / 80	$59,359	$62,805
2048	81 / 81	$60,665	$64,186
2049	82 / 82	$61,999	$65,598
2050	83 / 83	$63,363	$67,042
2051	84 / 84	$64,757	$68,517
2052	85 / 85	$66,182	$70,024
2053	86 / 86	$67,638	$71,564

Year	Ages/Event	Matthew	Mary
2054	87 / 87	$69,126	$73,139
2055	88 / 88	$70,647	$74,748
2056	89 / 89	$72,201	$76,392
2057	90 / 90	$73,790	$78,073
2058	Matthew's Plan Ends	$75,413	$79,791
2059	- / 92		$81,546
2060	Mary's Plan Ends		$83,340

Notes

Assumption for Cost of Living Adjustment (COLA) is 2.20% annually.

See Important Disclosure Information section in this Report for explanations of assumptions, limitations, methodologies, and a glossary.

Worksheet Detail - Health Care Expense Schedule

Scenario : What If 1

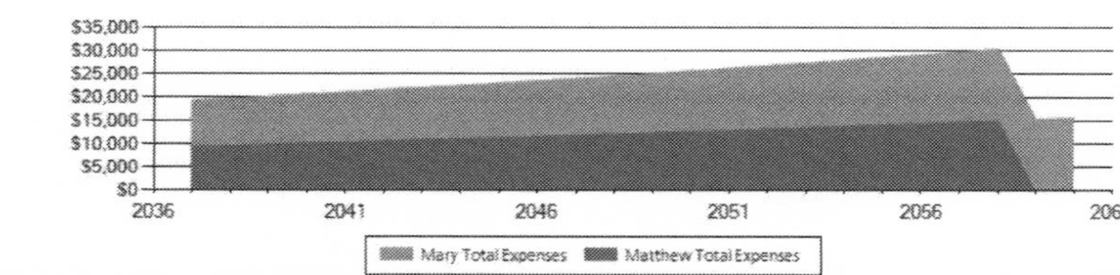

Year	Age/Event	Matthew						Mary						Annual Total
		Private Insurance Prior to Medicare	Medicare Part B	Medicare Part D	Medigap Policy	Out-of-Pocket	Matthew's Total	Private Insurance Prior to Medicare	Medicare Part B	Medicare Part D	Medigap Policy	Out-of-Pocket	Mary's Total	
2037	Both retire and start Medicare	$0	$2,431	$885	$3,609	$2,831	$9,755	$0	$2,431	$885	$3,289	$2,831	$9,436	$19,191
2038	71/71	$0	$2,485	$904	$3,688	$2,893	$9,970	$0	$2,485	$904	$3,361	$2,893	$9,643	$19,613
2039	72/72	$0	$2,540	$924	$3,769	$2,956	$10,189	$0	$2,540	$924	$3,435	$2,956	$9,855	$20,044
2040	73/73	$0	$2,595	$944	$3,852	$3,022	$10,413	$0	$2,595	$944	$3,511	$3,022	$10,072	$20,485
2041	74/74	$0	$2,653	$965	$3,937	$3,088	$10,642	$0	$2,653	$965	$3,588	$3,088	$10,294	$20,936
2042	75/75	$0	$2,711	$986	$4,023	$3,156	$10,876	$0	$2,711	$986	$3,667	$3,156	$10,520	$21,397
2043	76/76	$0	$2,771	$1,008	$4,112	$3,225	$11,116	$0	$2,771	$1,008	$3,748	$3,225	$10,752	$21,867
2044	77/77	$0	$2,831	$1,030	$4,202	$3,296	$11,360	$0	$2,831	$1,030	$3,830	$3,296	$10,988	$22,348
2045	78/78	$0	$2,894	$1,053	$4,295	$3,369	$11,610	$0	$2,894	$1,053	$3,914	$3,369	$11,230	$22,840
2046	79/79	$0	$2,957	$1,076	$4,389	$3,443	$11,866	$0	$2,957	$1,076	$4,001	$3,443	$11,477	$23,343
2047	80/80	$0	$3,022	$1,100	$4,486	$3,519	$12,127	$0	$3,022	$1,100	$4,089	$3,519	$11,729	$23,856
2048	81/81	$0	$3,089	$1,124	$4,585	$3,596	$12,394	$0	$3,089	$1,124	$4,179	$3,596	$11,987	$24,381
2049	82/82	$0	$3,157	$1,149	$4,685	$3,675	$12,666	$0	$3,157	$1,149	$4,270	$3,675	$12,251	$24,917
2050	83/83	$0	$3,226	$1,174	$4,789	$3,756	$12,945	$0	$3,226	$1,174	$4,364	$3,756	$12,521	$25,465

See Important Disclosure Information section in this Report for explanations of assumptions, limitations, methodologies, and a glossary.

Prepared for : Matthew and Mary Client | Company: Raymond James | Prepared by: Mark Aho

03/20/2018 | Page 23 of 29

Worksheet Detail - Health Care Expense Schedule

Scenario : What If 1

Year	Age/Event	Matthew						Mary						Annual Total
		Private Insurance Prior to Medicare	Medicare Part B	Medicare Part D	Medigap Policy	Out-of-Pocket	Matthew's Total	Private Insurance Prior to Medicare	Medicare Part B	Medicare Part D	Medigap Policy	Out-of-Pocket	Mary's Total	
2051	84/84	$0	$3,297	$1,200	$4,894	$3,839	$13,230	$0	$3,297	$1,200	$4,460	$3,839	$12,796	$26,026
2052	85/85	$0	$3,370	$1,226	$5,002	$3,923	$13,521	$0	$3,370	$1,226	$4,559	$3,923	$13,078	$26,598
2053	86/86	$0	$3,444	$1,253	$5,112	$4,009	$13,818	$0	$3,444	$1,253	$4,659	$4,009	$13,365	$27,183
2054	87/87	$0	$3,520	$1,281	$5,224	$4,098	$14,122	$0	$3,520	$1,281	$4,761	$4,098	$13,659	$27,782
2055	88/88	$0	$3,597	$1,309	$5,339	$4,188	$14,433	$0	$3,597	$1,309	$4,866	$4,188	$13,960	$28,393
2056	89/89	$0	$3,676	$1,338	$5,456	$4,280	$14,750	$0	$3,676	$1,338	$4,973	$4,280	$14,267	$29,017
2057	90/90	$0	$3,757	$1,367	$5,576	$4,374	$15,075	$0	$3,757	$1,367	$5,083	$4,374	$14,581	$29,656
2058	Matthew's plan ends	$0	$3,840	$1,397	$5,699	$4,470	$15,406	$0	$3,840	$1,397	$5,194	$4,470	$14,902	$30,308
2059	-/92	$0	$0	$0	$0	$0	$0	$0	$3,924	$1,428	$5,309	$4,569	$15,230	$15,230
2060	Mary's plan ends	$0	$0	$0	$0	$0	$0	$0	$4,011	$1,459	$5,425	$4,669	$15,565	$15,565
Total Lifetime Cost of Health Care				**$272,284**						**$294,157**				

Notes

- Program assumptions:
  - The scenario assumes that client and co-client will each use a combination of Medicare Part A (Hospital Insurance), Part B (Medical Insurance), Part D (Prescription Drug Insurance), Medigap insurance , and Out-of Pocket expenses. The program uses initial default values that may have been adjusted based on your preferences and information provided by you.
  - The scenario assumes that client and co-client each qualify to receive Medicare Part A at no charge and therefore it is not reflected in the Health Care Expense schedule.
  - Estimates for private insurance prior to retirement are based on the information you provided.
  - Medicare and Medigap costs begin at the later of age 65, your retirement age, or the current year.
- All costs are in future dollars.
- Costs associated with Long Term Care needs are not addressed by this goal. A separate LTC goal can be created.
- General Information regarding Medicare:
  - Part B premiums are uniform nationally and are increased for those with a higher Modified Adjusted Gross Income.
  - Part D coverage is optional. Premiums are increased for those with a higher Modified Adjusted Gross Income, differ from state to state, and vary based on the specific plan and level of benefit selected.
  - Medigap coverage is optional and policies (Plans A-N) are issued by private insurers.
  - Clients may incur out-of-pocket healthcare expenses, for costs not covered by Medicare benefits and Medigap insurance.
  - If clients retire before age 65, they may choose to purchase private health insurance or to self-insure. Costs and coverage for private health insurance varies greatly.

See Important Disclosure Information section in this Report for explanations of assumptions, limitations, methodologies, and a glossary.

Star Track

Star Track History

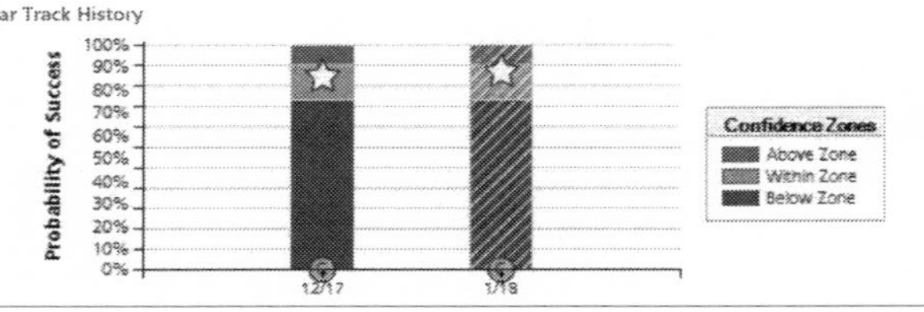

The Star Track History graph illustrates the progress you've made toward attaining your Goals over time. Each bar reflects the projected results of your Recommended Plan, as recorded on the date indicated. Data in each bar can differ substantially in assets included, goal values, and other underlying data. Patterned bars, if shown, were created automatically and may reflect asset values that were not fully updated.

The ☆ shows the Probability of Success for your Recommended Scenario.

The ◉ shows the Probability of Success for your Current Scenario.

Total Goal Spending

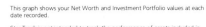

Total Spending: $3,100,000 · $2,480,000 · $1,860,000 · $1,240,000 · $620,000 · $0 — 12/17 · 1/18

Goal Spending: Recommended · Current

The Total Goal Spending graph provides a quick view of how your Goals have changed over time. The graph plots the Total Goal Spending required to fund all of your Goals. Each set of data points corresponds to a bar in the Star Track History graph above.

The ☆ shows the Total Goal Spending for your Recommended Scenario.

The ◉ shows the Total Goal Spending for your Current Scenario.

Net Worth and Investment Portfolio

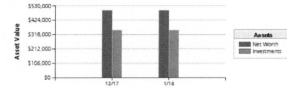

Asset Value: $530,000 · $424,000 · $318,000 · $212,000 · $106,000 · $0 — 12/17 · 1/18

Assets: Net Worth · Investments

This graph shows your Net Worth and Investment Portfolio values at each date recorded.

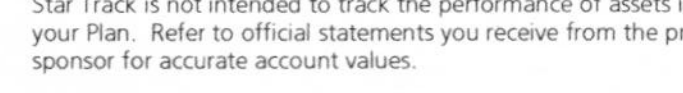

Star Track is not intended to track the performance of assets included in your Plan. Refer to official statements you receive from the product sponsor for accurate account values.

See Important Disclosure Information section in this Report for explanations of assumptions, limitations, methodologies, and a glossary.

Prepared for : Matthew and Mary Client | Company: Raymond James | Prepared by: Mark Aho

03/20/2018 | Page 25 of 29

Glossary

Asset Allocation

Asset Allocation is the process of determining what portions of your portfolio holdings are to be invested in the various asset classes.

Asset Class

Asset Class is a standard term that broadly defines a category of investments. The three basic asset classes are Cash, Bonds, and Stocks. Bonds and Stocks are often further subdivided into more narrowly defined classes. Some of the most common asset classes are defined below.

Cash and Cash Alternatives

Cash typically includes bank accounts or certificates of deposit, which are insured by the Federal Deposit Insurance Corporation up to a limit per account. Cash Alternatives typically include money market securities, U.S. treasury bills, and other investments that are readily convertible to cash, have a stable market value, and a very short-term maturity. U.S. Treasury bills are backed by the full faith and credit of the U.S. Government and, when held to maturity, provide safety of principal. (See the "Risks Inherent in Investing" section in this Important Disclosure Information for a summary of the risks associated with investing in cash alternatives.)

Commodities

A commodity is food, metal, or another fixed physical substance that investors buy or sell, usually via futures contracts, and generally traded in very large quantities.

Bonds

Bonds are either domestic (U.S.) or global debt securities issued by either private corporations or governments. (See the "Risks Inherent in Investing" section in this Important Disclosure Information for a summary of the risks associated with investing in bonds. Bonds are also called "fixed income securities.")

Domestic government bonds are backed by the full faith and credit of the U.S. Government and have superior liquidity and, when held to maturity, safety of principal. Domestic corporate bonds carry the credit risk of their issuers and thus usually offer additional yield. Domestic government and corporate bonds can be sub-divided based upon their term to maturity. Short-term bonds have an approximate term to maturity of 1 to 5 years; intermediate-term bonds have an approximate term to maturity of 5 to 10 years; and, long-term bonds have an approximate term to maturity greater than 10 years.

Stocks

Stocks are equity securities of domestic and foreign corporations. (See the "Risks Inherent in Investing" section in this Important Disclosure Information for a summary of the risks associated with investing in stocks.)

Domestic stocks are equity securities of U.S. corporations. Domestic stocks are often sub-divided based upon the market capitalization of the company (the market value of the company's stock). "Large cap" stocks are from larger companies, "mid cap" from the middle range of companies, and "small cap" from smaller, perhaps newer, companies. Generally, small cap stocks experience greater market volatility than stocks of companies with larger capitalization. Small cap stocks are generally those from companies whose capitalization is less than $500 million, mid cap stocks those between $500 million and $5 billion, and large cap over $5 billion.

Large cap, mid cap and small cap may be further sub-divided into "growth" and "value" categories. Growth companies are those with an orientation towards growth, often characterized by commonly used metrics such as higher price-to-book and price-to-earnings ratios. Analogously, value companies are those with an orientation towards value, often characterized by commonly used metrics such as lower price-to-book and price-to-earnings ratios.

International stocks are equity securities from foreign corporations. International stocks are often sub-divided into those from "developed" countries and those from "emerging markets." The emerging markets are in less developed countries with emerging economies that may be characterized by lower income per capita, less developed infrastructure and nascent capital markets. These "emerging markets" usually are less economically and politically stable than the "developed markets." Investing in international stocks involves special risks, among which include foreign exchange volatility and risks of investing under different tax, regulatory and accounting standards.

Asset Mix

Asset Mix is the combination of asset classes within a portfolio, and is usually expressed as a percentage for each asset class.

Bear Market Loss

The Bear Market Loss shows how a portfolio would have been impacted during the Great Recession (November 2007 through February 2009) or the Bond Bear Market (July 1979 through February 1980). The Bear Market Loss shows: 1) either the Great Recession Return or the Bond Bear Market Return, whichever is lower, and 2) the potential loss, if you had been invested in this cash-bond-stock-alternative portfolio during the period with the lower return. See Great Recession Return and Bond Bear Market Return.

Glossary

Bear Market Test

The Bear Market Test, included in the Stress Tests, examines the impact on your Plan results if a Bear Market Loss occurred this year. The Bear Market Test shows the likelihood that you could fund your Needs, Wants and Wishes after experiencing such an event. See Bear Market Loss.

Bond Bear Market Return

The Bond Bear Market Return is the rate of return for a cash-bond-stock-alternative portfolio during the Bond Bear Market (July 1979 through February 1980), the worst bear market for bonds since the Great Depression. Goal Planning & Monitoring shows a Bond Bear Market Return for your Current, Risk-based, and Target Portfolios, calculated using historical returns of four broad-based asset class indices. See Great Recession Return.

Bypass Trust

An estate planning device used to pass down assets after death without subjecting them to the estate tax.

Cash Receipt Schedule

A Cash Receipt Schedule consists of one or more years of future after-tax amounts received from the anticipated sale of an Other Asset, exercising of Stock Options grants, or proceeds from Restricted Stock grants.

Concentrated Position

A Concentrated Position is when your portfolio contains a significant amount (as a percentage of the total portfolio value) in individual stock or bonds. Concentrated Positions have the potential to increase the risk of your portfolio.

Confidence Zone

See Monte Carlo Confidence Zone.

Current Dollars

The Results of Goal Planning & Monitoring calculations are in Future Dollars. To help you compare dollar amounts in different years, we also express the Results in Current Dollars, calculated by discounting the Future Dollars by the sequence of inflation rates used in the Plan.

Current Portfolio

Your Current Portfolio is comprised of all the investment assets you currently own (or a subset of your assets, based on the information you provided for this Plan), categorized by Asset Class and Asset Mix.

Fund All Goals

Fund All Goals is one of two ways for your assets and retirement income to be used to fund your goals. The other is Earmark, which means that an asset or retirement income is assigned to one or more goals, and will be used only for those goals. Fund All Goals means that the asset or income is not earmarked to fund specific goals, and can be used to fund any goal, as needed in the calculations.

Future Dollars

Future Dollars are inflated dollars. The Results of Goal Planning & Monitoring calculations are in Future Dollars. To help you compare dollar amounts in different years, we discount the Future Dollar amounts by the inflation rates used in the calculations and display the Results in the equivalent Current Dollars.

Great Recession Return

The Great Recession Return is the rate of return for a cash-bond-stock-alternative portfolio during the Great Recession (November 2007 through February 2009), the worst bear market for stocks since the Great Depression. Goal Planning & Monitoring shows a Great Recession Return for your Current, Risk-based, and Target Portfolios, calculated using historical returns of four broad-based asset class indices. See Bond Bear Market Return.

Inflation Rate

Inflation is the percentage increase in the cost of goods and services for a specified time period. A historical measure of inflation is the Consumer Price Index (CPI). In Goal Planning & Monitoring, the Inflation Rate is selected by your advisor, and can be adjusted in different scenarios.

Irrevocable Life Insurance Trust

An irrevocable trust set up with a life insurance policy as the asset, allowing the grantor of the policy to exempt the asset away from his or her taxable estate.

Liquidity

Liquidity is the ease with which an investment can be converted into cash.

Monte Carlo Confidence Zone

The Monte Carlo Confidence Zone is the range of probabilities that you (and/or your advisor) have selected as your target range for the Monte Carlo Probability of Success in your Plan. The Confidence Zone reflects the Monte Carlo Probabilities of Success with which you would be comfortable, based upon your Plan, your specific time horizon, risk profile, and other factors unique to you.

Glossary

Monte Carlo Probability of Success / Probability of Failure

The Monte Carlo Probability of Success is the percentage of trials of your Plan that were successful. If a Monte Carlo simulation runs your Plan 1,000 times, and if 600 of those runs are successful (i.e., all your goals are funded and you have at least $1 of Safety Margin), then the Probability of Success for that Plan, with all its underlying assumptions, would be 60%, and the Probability of Failure would be 40%.

Monte Carlo Simulations

Monte Carlo simulations are used to show how variations in rates of return each year can affect your results. A Monte Carlo simulation calculates the results of your Plan by running it many times, each time using a different sequence of returns. Some sequences of returns will give you better results, and some will give you worse results. These multiple trials provide a range of possible results, some successful (you would have met all your goals) and some unsuccessful (you would not have met all your goals).

Needs / Wants / Wishes

In Goal Planning & Monitoring, you choose an importance level from 10 to 1 (where 10 is the highest) for each of your financial goals. Then, the importance levels are divided into three groups: Needs, Wants, and Wishes. Needs are the goals that you consider necessary for your lifestyle, and are the goals that you must fulfill. Wants are the goals that you would really like to fulfill, but could live without. Wishes are the "dream goals" that you would like to fund, although you won't be too dissatisfied if you can't fund them. In Goal Planning & Monitoring, Needs are your most important goals, then Wants, then Wishes.

Portfolio Set

A Portfolio Set is a group of portfolios that provides a range of risk and return strategies for different investors.

Portfolio Total Return

A Portfolio Total Return is determined by weighting the return assumption for each Asset Class according to the Asset Mix.

Probability of Success / Probability of Failure

See Monte Carlo Probability of Success / Probability of Failure.

Real Return

The Real Return is the Total Return of your portfolio minus the Inflation Rate.

Recommended Scenario

The Recommended Scenario is the scenario selected by your advisor to be shown on the Results page and in Play Zone.

Retirement Start Date

For married couples, retirement in Goal Planning & Monitoring begins when both the client and spouse are retired. For single, divorced, or widowed clients, retirement begins when the client retires.

Risk

Risk is the chance that the actual return of an investment, asset class, or portfolio will be different from its expected or average return.

Risk-based Portfolio

The risk-based portfolio is the Model Portfolio associated with the risk score you selected.

Safety Margin

The Safety Margin is the hypothetical portfolio value at the end of the Plan. A Safety Margin of zero indicates the portfolio was depleted before the Plan ended.

Standard Deviation

Standard Deviation is a statistical measure of the volatility of an investment, an asset class, or a portfolio. It measures the degree by which an actual return might vary from the average return, or mean. Typically, the higher the standard deviation, the higher the potential risk of the investment, asset class, or portfolio.

Star Track

Star Track provides a summary of your Plan results over time, using a bar graph. Each bar shows the Monte Carlo Probability of Success for your Recommended Scenario, on the date specified, compared to the Monte Carlo Probability of Success for a scenario using all Target values.

Target Band

The Target Band is the portfolio(s) that could be appropriate for you, based upon the risk-based portfolio.

Target Goal Amount

The Target Goal Amount is the amount you would expect to spend, or the amount you would like to spend, for each financial goal.

Glossary

Target Portfolio

Target Portfolio is the portfolio you have selected based upon your financial goals and your risk tolerance.

Target Retirement Age

Target Retirement Age is the age at which you would like to retire.

Target Savings Amount

In the Resources section of Goal Planning & Monitoring, you enter the current annual additions being made to your investment assets. The total of these additions is your Target Savings Amount.

Time Horizon

Time Horizon is the period from now until the time the assets in this portfolio will begin to be used.

Total Return

Total Return is an assumed, hypothetical growth rate for a specified time period. The Total Return is either (1) the Portfolio Total Return or (2) as entered by you or your advisor. Also see "Real Return."

Wants

See "Needs / Wants / Wishes".

Willingness

In Goal Planning & Monitoring, in addition to specifying Target Goal Amounts, a Target Savings Amount, and Target Retirement Ages, you also specify a Willingness to adjust these Target values. The Willingness choices are Very Willing, Somewhat Willing, Slightly Willing, and Not at All.

Wishes

See "Needs / Wants / Wishes".

Plan Delivery Acknowledgement

This plan should be reviewed periodically to ensure that the decisions made continue to be appropriate, particularly if there are changes in family circumstances including, but not limited to an inheritance, birth of a child, death of a family member, or material change in incomes or expenses.

We (Matthew and Mary Client) have reviewed and accept the information contained within this plan and understand the assumptions associated with it. We believe that all information provided by us is complete and accurate to the best of our knowledge. We recognize that performance is not guaranteed and that all future projections are included simply as a tool for decision making and do not represent a forecast of our financial future.

Your advisor (Mark Aho) will review this plan with you on a periodic basis to determine whether your stated goals and assumptions in this plan are still relevant. It is not expected that the plan will change frequently. In particular, short-term changes in the financial markets should not generally require adjustments to the plan. It is your obligation to notify all interested parties of any material changes that would alter the objectives of this plan. If all interested parties are not notified of any material changes, then the current plan document would become invalid.

____

Client signature & date

____

Advisor signature & date

____

Delivery Date

Notes

We have prepared this plan based on information provided by you. We have not attempted to verify the accuracy or completeness of this information. As the future cannot be forecast with certainty, actual results will vary from these projections. It is possible that these variations may be material. The degree of uncertainty normally increases with the length of the future period covered.

Financial Advisor : Mark Aho

Plan Name : Financial Goal Plan
Report Name : Financial Goal Plan 03/20/2018

Appendix 2

Ownership Ledger

About the Author

MARK A. AHO is a devoted husband, a dedicated father, and a successful financial advisor in the Upper Peninsula of Michigan. He holds an MBA, CFP®, and CIMA® and has an infectious optimism and zest for life. He feels blessed to have been adopted as an infant and raised by loving parents, and he has always embraced the noble notions of faith and family.

Made in the USA
Middletown, DE
14 December 2019

80401290R00142